Exploring Mediterranean Diet

A Beginner's Cookbook. Initiate Your Journey to Wellness with Delectable, Wholesome Recipes and Pro Tips for Embracing the Mediterranean Lifestyle

MIRA GREEN

TABLE OF CONTENTS

CHAPTER 1: INTRODUCTION 1
    Health Benefits Associated with the Mediterranean Lifestyle 4
    Core Principles and Fundamentals 5
    Tips for Grocery Shopping with a Mediterranean Focus 8

CHAPTER 2: BREAKFAST AND BRUNCH 11
    Egg Sandwiches with Rosemary, Tomato & Feta 13
    Mozzarella, Basil & Zucchini Frittata 15
    Spinach & Egg Scramble with Raspberries 17
    Cauliflower Crust Breakfast Pizza 19
    Vegetable Omelets 21
    Salmon Hash With Sunny-Side-Up Eggs 23
    Berry-Almond Smoothie Bowl 25
    Shakshuka 27
    Sheet-Pan Chickpeas and Eggs 29
    Sheet-Pan Greens and Feta Frittata 31
    Steak, Egg, and Goat Cheese Pizza 33
    Mediterranean Breakfast Sandwiches 35
    Breakfast Ham and Egg Cups 37
    Asparagus and Prosciutto Frittata 39
    Greek Vegetable and Feta Cheese Pie (Spanakopita) 41
    Spanish-style Tomatoes on Toast 43
    Oatmeal with Yogurt and Nutmeg 45
    Turkish Eggs with Greek Yogurt (Cilbir) 47

    The Best Protein Oatmeal (With Quick Oats) 49

    Labneh Pita Sandwich 51

CHAPTER 3: LUNCH 53

    Pesto Chicken Quinoa Bowls 55

    Tomato & Avocado Cheese Sandwich 57

    Piled-High Vegetable Pitas 59

    Cucumber-Chicken Green Goddess Wrap 61

    Mediterranean Pasta Salad 63

    Vegetarian Protein Bowl 65

    Roasted Salmon Rice Bowl with Beets & Brussels 67

    Mediterranean Vegetable Soup 69

    3-Ingredient Roasted Red Pepper Soup with Chickpeas 71

    Chicken & Cucumber Pita Sandwiches with Yogurt Sauce 73

    Slow-Cooker Chicken & Chickpea Soup 75

    Prosciutto, Mozzarella & Melon Plate 77

    Ravioli & Vegetable Soup 78

    Tuna & Olive Spinach Salad 80

    Meal-Prep Roasted Vegetable Bowls with Pesto 82

    Greek Chicken and Rice Skillet 84

    Mini Chicken Shawarma 86

    15-Minute Mediterranean Couscous With Tuna And Pepperoncini 88

    Pesto Quinoa Bowls With Roasted Veggies And Labneh 90

    15-Minute Mezze Plate With Toasted Za'atar Pita Bread 92

CHAPTER 4: DINNER 95

    Walnut-Rosemary Crusted Salmon 97

Charred Shrimp, Pesto & Quinoa Bowls 99

Sheet-Pan Salmon with Sweet Potatoes & Broccoli 101

Prosciutto Pizza with Corn & Arugula 103

Eggplant Parmesan 105

BBQ Shrimp with Garlicky Kale & Parmesan-Herb Couscous 107

Mediterranean Chicken 110

Feta, Spinach & Tomato Stuffed Salmon 112

Roasted Tomatoes 114

One-Pan Tuna Pasta 116

Caprese Asparagus 118

Feta & Herb Crusted Salmon 120

Halloumi Salad 122

Gigantes Plaki (Greek Baked Beans) 124

Baked Chorizo and Squash Rice with Manchego Crust 126

Spicy Merguez and Cod Tray Roast 128

Italian Baked Meatballs 130

Lamb Tagine 132

Chicken Parmesan 134

Mediterranean Tilapia 136

Favorite Meat Loaf Gyros 138

Mediterranean Tomato Bites 140

CHAPTER 5: DESSERTS AND SWEETS 143

Loukoumades – Greek Honey Balls 145

Best Tahini Brownies 147

Olive Oil Cake 149

Greek Yogurt Panna Cotta 151

Brûléed Ricotta 153
Honeyed Phyllo Stacks with Pistachios, Spiced Fruit & Yogurt 155
Sticky Gluten-Free Lemon Cake 157
Red Fruit Salad with Lemon-Vanilla Bean Syrup 159
Crema Catalana 161
Galaktoboureko 163

Chapter 1: Introduction

Welcome to the heart of Mediterranean cuisine, a culinary journey that transcends food to embrace a lifestyle rooted in health, history, and the simple joy of savoring every bite. The Mediterranean diet, hailed as one of the world's healthiest, reflects the traditional eating patterns of countries bordering the Mediterranean Sea.

Introduction to the Mediterranean Lifestyle: The Mediterranean diet is not just about what's on your plate; it's a holistic approach to well-being. It draws inspiration from the dietary habits of Greece, Italy, Spain, and other Mediterranean countries, emphasizing fresh, whole foods and mindful eating practices.

Core Principles: At its core, the Mediterranean diet is a celebration of simplicity and balance. Rich in fruits, vegetables, whole grains, lean proteins, and heart-healthy fats, this diet minimizes processed foods and added sugars. Olive oil, a staple in Mediterranean kitchens, takes center stage, providing exquisite flavors and numerous health benefits.

Culinary Traditions and Diversity: Dive into the diverse culinary traditions that define the Mediterranean diet. From the robust flavors of Greek salads to the aromatic spices of Italian pasta dishes, each region contributes to a tapestry of tastes that delight the senses.

Health Benefits: The Mediterranean diet has been associated with several health advantages via numerous research. Its focus on nutrient-dense foods has been linked to a decreased risk of diabetes, heart disease, and several types of cancer. Additionally, the inclusion of olive oil and omega-3-rich fish supports cognitive health.

Sustainable Practices: Beyond its impact on personal health, the Mediterranean diet embraces sustainable practices. Locally sourced, seasonal ingredients are prioritized, reflecting an appreciation for the environment and a connection to the land.

Embark on a Journey: As we embark on this culinary journey through the Mediterranean diet, let's explore the foundations of this timeless way of eating. From the sun-drenched fields to the azure coastlines, discover the secrets to a healthier and more flavorful life inspired by the Mediterranean lifestyle.

HEALTH BENEFITS ASSOCIATED WITH THE MEDITERRANEAN LIFESTYLE

The Mediterranean lifestyle goes beyond a mere diet; it's a holistic approach to well-being linked to many health benefits. As we embrace this way of life, let's delve into the remarkable advantages of adopting the Mediterranean diet and lifestyle.

Heart Health: At the core of the Mediterranean lifestyle is a heart-healthy approach to eating. The diet is renowned for promoting cardiovascular well-being, with studies suggesting a lower risk of heart disease. Adding olive oil, abundant in monounsaturated fats, is pivotal in maintaining healthy cholesterol levels.

Reduced Risk of Chronic Diseases: The Mediterranean lifestyle has been associated with a decreased risk of chronic diseases, including type 2 diabetes and certain cancers. The emphasis on antioxidant-rich fruits, vegetables, and whole grains contributes to overall health and resilience against illness.

Weight Management: Those who follow the Mediterranean lifestyle often find it conducive to weight management. Focusing on nutrient-dense foods, portion control, and the consumption of satisfying, whole foods helps maintain a healthy weight without the need for restrictive measures.

Brain Health and Cognitive Function: The Mediterranean diet's positive impact extends to cognitive health. Rich in omega-3 fatty acids from fish, along with antioxidants from fruits and vegetables, the diet is thought to support brain function and lower the chance of cognitive deterioration as people get older.

Inflammation Reduction: Chronic inflammation contributes to various health issues, and the Mediterranean lifestyle aims to mitigate this risk. The diet's emphasis on anti-inflammatory foods, such as fatty fish, nuts, and olive oil, supports the body in managing inflammation.

Longevity: Regions following the Mediterranean lifestyle have notably high rates of centenarians, individuals who live to be 100 years old or older. While various factors influence longevity, the Mediterranean diet's nutrient-rich, balanced nature likely contributes to its practitioners' overall health and well-being.

Emotional Well-being: The Mediterranean lifestyle strongly emphasizes enjoying meals with family and friends. This communal aspect of dining, combined with the pleasure of savoring wholesome, flavorful foods, fosters a positive relationship with eating and contributes to emotional well-being.

Conclusion: As we explore the health benefits associated with the Mediterranean lifestyle, it becomes clear that this approach to eating is not just about nourishing the body; it's about fostering a harmonious and fulfilling connection between our choices and overall health. Let's continue this journey, embracing the profound advantages of Mediterranean living.

CORE PRINCIPLES AND FUNDAMENTALS

Understanding the core principles of the Mediterranean lifestyle and the fundamentals that form the backbone of this celebrated way of life is essential. At its heart, the Mediterranean diet is not just a set of dietary guidelines; it's a philosophy that intertwines food, culture, and a profound appreciation for a life well-lived.

- **Emphasis on Whole, Plant-Based Foods:** Central to the Mediterranean way of eating is focusing on whole, minimally processed foods. Load your plate with abundant fresh fruits, vegetables, whole grains, legumes, nuts, and seeds. These nutrient-rich choices provide the foundation for a nourished and resilient body.
- **Heart-Healthy Fats - Olive Oil:** Olive oil is the cornerstone of Mediterranean cuisine. Rich in monounsaturated fats and antioxidants, it not only enhances the flavors of dishes but also contributes to heart health. Drizzle, dip, and savor the liquid gold that is olive oil.
- **Moderate Consumption of Fish and Lean Proteins:** Seafood, particularly fatty fish like salmon and sardines, is a regular feature of the Mediterranean diet. With omega-3 fatty acids promoting cardiovascular health, fish is prominent alongside lean proteins like poultry and legumes.
- **Mindful Eating Practices:** In the Mediterranean, meals are not merely a means of sustenance; they are moments to be cherished. Adopt mindful eating practices by savoring each bite, appreciating the flavors, and engaging in the communal joy of shared meals with family and friends.
- **Red Wine in Moderation:** A symbol of conviviality, red wine, when consumed in moderation, is a part of the Mediterranean lifestyle. Rich in antioxidants, red wine is thought to offer cardiovascular benefits. However, moderation remains vital to reaping its potential advantages.
- **Local and Seasonal Ingredients:** Connect with the land by embracing local and seasonal ingredients. This supports sustainable practices and ensures your meals are vibrant, fresh, and harmonized with the changing seasons.
- **Balancing Macronutrients:** Achieve a harmonious balance of macronutrients - carbohydrates, proteins, and fats. The Mediterranean diet prioritizes healthy fats, complex carbohydrates, and moderate protein intake, providing a well-rounded nutritional profile.
- **Social Interaction and Enjoyment:** Eating is a social affair in the Mediterranean. Cultivate a sense of enjoyment and connection by sharing meals with loved ones. The communal aspect of dining contributes to overall well-being and enhances the pleasure derived from food.

As we delve into the core principles and fundamentals, let's not view the Mediterranean lifestyle as a set of rules but as an invitation to savor life's flavors with intention, gratitude, and a profound sense of joy.

TIPS FOR GROCERY SHOPPING WITH A MEDITERRANEAN FOCUS

Embarking on a journey into the heart of Mediterranean cuisine begins at the grocery store, where the vibrant colors and enticing aromas of fresh, wholesome ingredients await. Navigate the aisles with confidence and purpose as you adopt these tips for grocery shopping with a Mediterranean focus.

- **Prioritize Fresh Produce:** Start your shopping expedition in the produce section. Load your cart with colorful fruits and vegetables, emphasizing seasonal and locally sourced options. The Mediterranean diet thrives on the earth's bounty, from juicy tomatoes to crisp greens.
- **Choose Whole Grains:** Navigate to the grains and cereals aisle with an eye for whole grains. Opt for staples like whole wheat couscous, quinoa, bulgur, and farro. These nutrient-rich grains form the base of many Mediterranean dishes, providing fiber and essential minerals.
- **Embrace Legumes:** Stock up on chickpeas, lentils, and cannellini beans. These protein-packed powerhouses are versatile ingredients that add heartiness to salads, soups, and stews—a key element in the Mediterranean diet.
- **Select Lean Proteins:** For proteins, lean towards poultry, fish, and seafood. Salmon, mackerel, and sardines, rich in omega-3 fatty acids, are excellent choices. Poultry, including chicken and turkey, provides a lean protein source for a balanced diet.
- **Dive into Dairy and Dairy Alternatives:** Choose Greek yogurt and feta cheese in the dairy aisle for their creamy textures and tangy flavors. Alternatively, explore dairy-free options such as almond or coconut-based yogurts.
- **Navigate the Olive Oil Aisle:** Olive oil is a star player in Mediterranean cooking. Take additional virgin olive oil for its vigorous flavor and inexhaustible wellbeing benefits. Consider trying different varieties to discover nuanced flavors that complement various dishes.
- **Visit the Fish Market:** If available, visit the fish market for fresh seafood. Consider incorporating a variety of fish into your diet experimenting with flavors and textures to diversify your meals.
- **Explore the Mediterranean Pantry:** Stock your pantry with essentials like capers, olives, artichokes, and sun-dried tomatoes. These flavorful additions enhance a range of dishes, adding depth and complexity to your culinary creations.

- **Incorporate Nuts and Seeds:** Include a variety of nuts and seeds in your shopping list. Almonds, walnuts, and chia seeds are fabulous choices, giving a crunchy surface and a boost of solid fats and supplements.
- **Read Labels Mindfully:** Read labels and choose minimally processed, wholesome products. Opt for items with simple ingredient lists, avoiding excessive additives and preservatives.

Armed with these tips, let your grocery shopping experience become a delightful exploration of Mediterranean flavors and a celebration of nourishing, healthful choices.

Chapter 2: Breakfast and Brunch

EGG SANDWICHES WITH ROSEMARY, TOMATO & FETA

Prep Time: 10 minutes
Cook Time: 10 minutes
Serves: 4

Ingredients:

- 4 large eggs
- 4 whole-grain English muffins, split and toasted
- 1 large tomato, thinly sliced
- 1/2 cup crumbled feta cheese
- Fresh rosemary, chopped
- Salt and pepper to taste
- Olive oil for cooking

Directions:

1. Prepare the Eggs:
- Beat the eggs in a bowl and add salt, pepper, and a small teaspoon of freshly chopped rosemary.
- Heat a non-stick skillet over medium heat and add olive oil.
- Transfer the whisked eggs to the skillet and gently stir until light, frothy curds form. Cook till the doneness you desire.

2. Assemble the Sandwiches:
- Take each toasted English muffin half and layer with a slice of tomato.
- Spoon a portion of the scrambled eggs onto the tomato slice.

3. Add Feta and More Rosemary:
- Sprinkle crumbled feta cheese over the eggs on each sandwich.
- Garnish with additional chopped fresh rosemary for an extra burst of flavor.

4. Close and Serve:
- Top each sandwich with half of the English muffin to create a delightful egg sandwich.

Nutrition Information (per serving)

Note: Nutritional values are approximate and may vary based on specific ingredients and quantities.)

- Calories: 280
- Protein: 16g
- Fat: 14g
- Carbohydrates: 24g
- Fiber: 4g
- Sugar: 3g
- Sodium: 450mg

MOZZARELLA, BASIL & ZUCCHINI FRITTATA

Prep Time: 15 minutes
Cook Time: 20 minutes
Serves: 4

Ingredients:

- 6 large eggs
- 1 medium zucchini, thinly sliced
- 1 cup fresh mozzarella, diced
- 1/4 cup fresh basil, chopped
- 1/2 onion, finely chopped
- 2 tablespoons olive oil
- Salt and pepper to taste
- Grated Parmesan cheese for garnish (optional)

Directions:

1. Preheat the Oven:
- Preheat your oven's broiler.

2. Saute Zucchini and Onion:
- Heat olive oil in an oven-safe skillet over medium heat.
- Add sliced zucchini and chopped onion. Saute until the vegetables are softened, about 5 minutes—season with salt and pepper.

3. Whisk Eggs:
- In a bowl, whisk the eggs until well beaten—season with salt and pepper.

4. Combine Eggs, Zucchini, and Basil:
- Pour the beaten eggs over the sautéed zucchini and onion in the skillet.
- Sprinkle diced mozzarella and chopped fresh basil evenly over the eggs.

5. Cook on the Stovetop:
- Cook on the stovetop over medium warm for approximately 5 minutes, permitting the edges to set.

6. Broil in the Oven:

- Transfer the skillet to the preheated oven and broil for 5-7 minutes or until the top is set and golden brown.

7. Finish and Serve:

- Carefully remove the skillet from the oven.
- Optionally, sprinkle grated Parmesan cheese over the frittata for extra flavor.
- Before cutting the frittata into wedges, let it cool somewhat.

Nutrition Information (per serving)

(Note: Nutritional values are approximate and may vary based on specific ingredients and quantities.)

- Calories: 250
- Protein: 15g
- Fat: 18g
- Carbohydrates: 5g
- Fiber: 1g
- Sugar: 3g
- Sodium: 350mg

SPINACH & EGG SCRAMBLE WITH RASPBERRIES

Prep Time: 10 minutes
Cook Time: 5 minutes
Serves: 2

Ingredients:

- 4 large eggs
- 2 cups fresh baby spinach
- 1/2 cup fresh raspberries
- 1/4 cup feta cheese, crumbled
- 1 tablespoon olive oil
- Salt and pepper to taste
- Fresh basil or mint for garnish (optional)

Directions:

1. **Prepare the Eggs:**

- Beat the eggs well in a basin. Add pepper and salt for seasoning.

2. **Cook Spinach:**

- Heat olive oil in a non-stick skillet over medium heat.
- Add the fresh baby spinach to the skillet and sauté until wilted.

3. **Add Eggs to the Skillet:**

- Pour the beaten eggs over the sautéed spinach in the skillet.

4. **Scramble the Eggs:**

- Gently scramble the eggs with the spinach, stirring occasionally until the eggs are fully cooked.

5. **Add Raspberries and Feta:**

- Once the eggs are almost set, add fresh raspberries and crumbled feta cheese to the skillet. Stir briefly to incorporate the ingredients.

6. Finish and Garnish:

- Continue cooking for another minute or until the raspberries are slightly softened.
- Garnish with fresh mint or basil.

7. Serve:

- Divide the Spinach & Egg Scramble onto plates.
- Enjoy your delightful and nutritious breakfast!

Nutrition Information (per serving)

(Note: Nutritional values are approximate and may vary based on specific ingredients and quantities.)

- Calories: 280
- Protein: 16g
- Fat: 20g
- Carbohydrates: 10g
- Fiber: 4g
- Sugar: 4g
- Sodium: 350mg

CAULIFLOWER CRUST BREAKFAST PIZZA

Prep Time: 10 minutes **Cook Time:** 10 minutes **Servings:** 2

Ingredients:

Cauliflower Crust:

- 1 medium head cauliflower, grated or riced
- 1 egg
- ½ cup shredded mozzarella cheese
- 2 tablespoons grated Parmesan cheese
- 1 teaspoon dried oregano
- ½ teaspoon garlic powder
- Salt and pepper to taste

Toppings:

- 4 slices of bacon, cooked and crumbled
- 4 large eggs
- ½ cup shredded cheddar cheese
- Chopped fresh parsley (optional, for garnish)

Directions:

1. Preparation:

- Set the oven's temperature to 400°F or 200°C.
- Prepare a baking sheet or pizza pan lined with parchment paper.

2. Cauliflower Crust:

- After grating or ricing the cauliflower, place it in a bowl that is safe to microwave for five to six minutes or until it is soft.
- After allowing the cauliflower to cool slightly, place it on a sanitized kitchen towel. Extract as much liquid as you can from the cauliflower.
- Combine the cauliflower, egg, shredded mozzarella, Parmesan cheese, oregano, salt, garlic powder, and pepper in a mixing dish.
- Blend until thoroughly blended.

- Deliver the cauliflower mixture onto the pizza pan or baking sheet that has been prepared. Form and spread into a circular crust that is about ¼ inch thick.

3. Baking the Crust:
- For 20 to 25 minutes, or until the crust is complex and the edges are golden brown, bake the cauliflower crust in the oven.
- After taking the crust out of the oven, let it cool somewhat. Turn the oven on again.

4. Assembling the Pizza:
- Evenly distribute the cheddar cheese shreds over the cauliflower crust.
- Create 4 small wells in the cheese, and crack one egg into each well.
- Distribute the cooked and crumbled bacon over the pizza, avoiding covering the eggs.

5. Final Baking:
- Place the pizza back in the oven and bake it for ten to fifteen minutes, or until the yolks are cooked to your desired consistency and the egg whites are set.
- After it's finished, take the pizza out of the oven and give it some time to cool.
- Garnish with chopped parsley if desired.

6. Serving
- Slice the cauliflower crust breakfast pizza into quarters and serve warm.

Nutritional Information (per serving):

- Calories: Approximately 280 kcal
- Total Fat: 18g
- Saturated Fat: 8g
- Carbohydrates: 7g
- Fiber: 3g
- Protein: 23g

VEGETABLE OMELETS

Prep Time: 10 minutes
Cook Time: 10 minutes
Serves: 2

Ingredients:

- 4 large eggs
- 1/2 bell pepper, diced (any color)
- 1/2 cup cherry tomatoes, halved
- 1/2 cup mushrooms, sliced
- 1/4 cup red onion, finely chopped
- 1/4 cup shredded cheese (cheddar, mozzarella, or your choice)
- 2 tablespoons fresh parsley, chopped
- Salt and pepper to taste
- 2 tablespoons olive oil

Directions:

1. Prepare Vegetables:

- Combine diced bell pepper, halved cherry tomatoes, sliced mushrooms, and finely chopped red onion in a bowl.

2. Whisk Eggs:

- In another bowl, whisk the eggs until well beaten—season with salt and pepper.

3. Cook Vegetables:

- Heat olive oil in a non-stick skillet over medium heat.
- Add the mixed vegetables to the skillet and sauté until slightly softened, about 3-4 minutes.

4. Pour Eggs Over Vegetables:

- Pour the beaten eggs evenly over the sautéed vegetables in the skillet.

5. Swirl and Cook:
- To make sure the eggs uniformly coat the veggies, swirl the skillet. Let the omelet cook without moving for a minute or until the edges are firm.

6. Add Cheese and Parsley:
- Sprinkle shredded cheese and chopped fresh parsley over one-half of the omelet.

7. Fold and Serve:
- Carefully fold the omelet in half, covering the cheese and parsley.
- Cook the omelet for two to three minutes or until it is cooked through and the cheese has melted.

8. Serve Warm:
- Slide the Vegetable Omelet onto a plate.
- Sprinkle more parsley on top, and serve it while it's still warm.

Nutrition Information (per serving)

(Note: Nutritional values are approximate and may vary based on specific ingredients and quantities.)

- Calories: 280
- Protein: 16g
- Fat: 20g
- Carbohydrates: 8g
- Fiber: 2g
- Sugar: 4g
- Sodium: 350mg

SALMON HASH WITH SUNNY-SIDE-UP EGGS

Prep Time: 15 minutes
Cook Time: 20 minutes
Serves: 4

Ingredients:

- 1 pound salmon fillet, cooked and flaked
- 4 cups potatoes, diced into small cubes
- 1 red bell pepper, diced
- 1 yellow onion, finely chopped
- 2 cloves garlic, minced
- 2 tablespoons olive oil
- 1 teaspoon smoked paprika
- 1 teaspoon dried thyme
- Salt and pepper to taste
- 4 large eggs
- Fresh parsley for garnish (optional)

Directions:

1. Prepare Salmon:

- Cook the salmon fillet using your preferred method (baking, grilling, or pan-searing). Once cooked, flake the salmon into bite-sized pieces.

2. Cook Potatoes:

- In a large skillet, preheat olive oil over medium heat.
- Add the diced potatoes and simmer for 10 to 12 minutes or until golden brown and crispy.

3. Add Vegetables:

- Toss the potatoes in a pan with chopped onion, minced garlic, and diced red bell pepper. Cook until the vegetables are softened.

4. Season the Hash:

- Sprinkle smoked paprika, dried thyme, salt, and pepper over the potato and vegetable mixture. Stir to combine.

5. Add Flaked Salmon:

- Gently fold in the flaked salmon, ensuring it is evenly distributed throughout the hash. Cook for an additional 3-5 minutes to heat the salmon.

6. Prepare Sunny-Side Up Eggs:

- To the desired doneness, cook the eggs sunny-side up in a separate nonstick pan.

7. Serve:

- Divide the salmon hash among serving plates.
- Top each portion with a sunny-side-up egg.

8. Garnish and Enjoy:

- Garnish with fresh parsley if desired.
- Serve immediately, and enjoy your Salmon Hash With Sunny-Side Eggs!

Nutrition Information (per serving)

(Note: Nutritional values are approximate and may vary based on specific ingredients and quantities.)

- Calories: 350
- Protein: 22g
- Fat: 18g
- Carbohydrates: 25g
- Fiber: 4g
- Sugar: 2g
- Sodium: 250mg

BERRY-ALMOND SMOOTHIE BOWL

Prep Time: 10 minutes
Cook Time: 0 minutes
Serves: 2

Ingredients:

- 1 cup mixed berries (strawberries, blueberries, raspberries)
- 1 frozen banana, sliced
- 1/2 cup Greek yogurt
- 1/4 cup almond butter
- 1/2 cup almond milk
- 1 tablespoon chia seeds
- 2 tablespoons sliced almonds
- Fresh mint leaves for garnish (optional)
- Honey or maple syrup for drizzling (optional)

Directions:

1. Blend the Smoothie Base:

- In a blender, combine frozen banana slices, Greek yogurt, almond butter, almond milk, and assorted berries.
- Blend until smooth and creamy.

2. Prepare the Toppings:

- Slice additional berries for topping.
- Mix chia seeds with a splash of almond milk in a small bowl and let it sit for a few minutes until it becomes like a gel.

3. Assemble the Smoothie Bowl:

- Pour the blended smoothie into bowls.

4. Add Toppings:

- If desired, top the smoothie bowls with sliced berries, chia seed pudding, sliced almonds, and fresh mint leaves.

5. **Drizzle with Honey (Optional):**
- If you like, drizzle honey or maple syrup over the top for added sweetness.

6. **Serve and Enjoy:**
- Serve and enjoy your delicious and nutritious Berry-Almond Smoothie Bowl!

Nutrition Information (per serving)

(Note: Nutritional values are approximate and may vary based on specific ingredients and quantities.)

- Calories: 300
- Protein: 10g
- Fat: 15g
- Carbohydrates: 35g
- Fiber: 8g
- Sugar: 18g
- Sodium: 100mg

SHAKSHUKA

Prep Time: 10 minutes
Cook Time: 20 minutes
Serves: 4

Ingredients:

- 2 tablespoons olive oil
- 1 onion, finely chopped
- 2 bell peppers, diced
- 3 cloves garlic, minced
- 1 teaspoon ground cumin
- 1 teaspoon ground paprika
- 1/2 teaspoon cayenne pepper (adjust to taste)
- 1 can (28 oz) crushed tomatoes
- Salt and pepper to taste
- 4-6 large eggs
- Fresh parsley or cilantro for garnish
- Feta cheese or crumbled goat cheese (optional)

Directions:

1. Saute Vegetables:

- Heat olive oil in a large skillet over medium heat. Add chopped onion and diced bell peppers. Saute until the vegetables are softened.

2. Add Spices:

- Stir in minced garlic, ground cumin, ground paprika, and cayenne pepper. Fry for another one to two minutes or until the spices are aromatic.

3. Pour in Crushed Tomatoes:

- Pour the crushed tomatoes into the skillet—season with salt and pepper to taste. Stir well to combine.

4. Simmer:

- Simmer for ten to fifteen minutes or until the sauce thickens.

5. Create Wells for Eggs:

- Using a spoon, create small wells in the tomato sauce. Crack an egg into each well.

6. Cook Eggs:

- Cover the skillet and let the eggs cook until the whites are set but the yolks are still runny about 5-7 minutes. If you prefer firmer yolks, cook a bit longer.

7. Garnish and Serve:

- Garnish the shakshuka with fresh parsley or cilantro. Optionally, crumble feta cheese or goat cheese over the top.

8. Serve Warm:

- Serve the shakshuka directly from the skillet. Scoop out portions with the eggs onto plates or shallow bowls.

Nutrition Information (per serving)

(Note: Nutritional values are approximate and may vary based on specific ingredients and quantities.)

- Calories: 220
- Protein: 10g
- Fat: 12g
- Carbohydrates: 20g
- Fiber: 5g
- Sugar: 10g
- Sodium: 400mg

SHEET-PAN CHICKPEAS AND EGGS

Prep Time: 15 minutes
Cook Time: 25 minutes
Serves: 4

Ingredients:

- Two cans (15 oz each) of rinsed and drained chickpeas
- 1 red bell pepper, diced
- 1 yellow bell pepper, diced
- 1 red onion, thinly sliced
- 4 cloves garlic, minced
- 2 teaspoons ground cumin
- 1 teaspoon smoked paprika
- 1/2 teaspoon chili powder
- 1/4 cup olive oil
- Salt and pepper to taste
- 4 large eggs
- Fresh parsley for garnish
- Optional: Feta cheese or crumbled goat cheese

Directions:

1. Preheat Oven:

- Preheat your oven to 425°F (220°C).

2. Prepare Chickpeas and Vegetables:

- Combine chickpeas, diced red and yellow bell peppers, sliced red onion, minced garlic, ground cumin, smoked paprika, olive oil, salt, chili powder, and pepper in a big bowl. Toss until well coated.

3. Spread on Sheet Pan:

- Spread the chickpea and vegetable mixture evenly on a sheet pan.

4. Roast in the Oven:

- Roast in the oven for about 20 minutes, stirring halfway through, or until the chickpeas are golden and the vegetables are tender.

5. Create Wells for Eggs:

- Make four small wells in the chickpea mixture using a spoon.

6. Crack Eggs onto Sheet Pan:

- Crack one egg into each well.

7. Continue Roasting:

- Place the sheet pan back in the oven and bake for five more minutes or until the yolks are still runny but the whites are firm.

8. Garnish and Serve:

- Garnish with fresh parsley and optional crumbled feta or goat cheese.

9. Serve Warm:

- Serve directly from the sheet pan. Scoop out portions with chickpeas, vegetables, and a perfectly baked egg.

Nutrition Information (per serving)

(Note: Nutritional values are approximate and may vary based on specific ingredients and quantities.)

- Calories: 320
- Protein: 16g
- Fat: 15g
- Carbohydrates: 30g
- Fiber: 8g
- Sugar: 6g
- Sodium: 450mg

SHEET-PAN GREENS AND FETA FRITTATA

Prep Time: 15 minutes
Cook Time: 25 minutes
Serves: 6

Ingredients:

- 10 large eggs
- 1 cup baby spinach, chopped
- 1 cup kale, stems removed and chopped
- 1/2 cup crumbled feta cheese
- 1/4 cup chopped fresh parsley
- 1/4 cup chopped green onions
- 1/4 cup milk
- 1 teaspoon olive oil
- Salt and pepper to taste
- Cooking spray for the sheet pan

Directions:

1. Preheat Oven:

- Turn on your oven and set the temperature to 375°F (190°C). Put a little bit of cooking spray on a sheet pan.

2. Prepare Greens:

- In a skillet, heat olive oil over medium heat. Add chopped spinach and kale. Cook the greens for 2-3 minutes until they are soft. Remove from heat and let them cool.

3. Whisk Eggs:

- Beat the eggs and milk together in a big bowl until mixed well. Add salt and pepper.

4. Combine Ingredients:

- Add the cooked and cooled greens, crumbled feta, chopped parsley, and green onions to the egg mixture. Stir gently to combine.

5. Pour into Sheet Pan:

- Pour the egg and greens mixture onto the prepared sheet pan, spreading it evenly.

6. Bake in the Oven:

- Bake in the oven for about 20-25 minutes or until the frittata is set in the center and the edges are golden brown.

7. Cool and Cut:

- Let the frittata cool a bit before cutting it into squares or wedges.

8. Serve Warm:

- Heat it and enjoy it for breakfast or brunch. It's tasty and good for you.

Nutrition Information (per serving)

(Note: Nutritional values are approximate and may vary based on specific ingredients and quantities.)

- Calories: 180
- Protein: 14g
- Fat: 12g
- Carbohydrates: 3g
- Fiber: 1g
- Sugar: 1g
- Sodium: 300mg

STEAK, EGG, AND GOAT CHEESE PIZZA

Prep Time: 15 minutes
Cook Time: 15 minutes
Serves: 4

Ingredients:

For the Pizza:

- 1 pound pizza dough (store-bought or homemade)
- 1/2 cup tomato sauce
- 1 cup shredded mozzarella cheese
- 4 ounces goat cheese, crumbled
- 1 cup cooked steak, thinly sliced
- 4 large eggs
- Salt and pepper to taste
- Fresh arugula for garnish (optional)

For the Steak Marinade:

- 1 tablespoon olive oil
- 2 cloves garlic, minced
- 1 teaspoon dried thyme
- Salt and pepper to taste

Directions:

1. Preheat Oven:
- Turn on your oven to the best temperature for your pizza dough.

2. Marinate the Steak:
- Mix olive oil, minced garlic, dried thyme, salt, and pepper in a bowl. Coat the steak slices with this marinade and set aside for at least 10 minutes.

3. Roll Out Pizza Dough:
- Roll out the pizza dough to the ideal thickness on a surface dusted with flour.

4. **Assemble Pizza:**
   - Put the flattened dough onto a pizza stone or baking sheet.
   - Put tomato sauce on the dough, but not to the edges.
   - Sprinkle shredded mozzarella cheese over the sauce.
   - Distribute the marinated and cooked steak slices evenly on the pizza.
   - Crumble goat cheese over the top.

5. **Bake the Pizza:**
   - Cook in the oven until the pizza crust is golden and the cheese is melted, following the instructions on the pizza dough.

6. **Cook Eggs:**
   - Fry the eggs in another pan.

7. **Add Sunny-Side Up Eggs:**
   - Once the pizza is done, carefully place the sunny-side-up eggs on top.

8. **Season and Garnish:**
   - Season the eggs with salt and pepper. Garnish the pizza with fresh arugula if desired.

9. **Serve Warm:**
   - Slice the pizza and serve it warm.

Nutrition Information (per serving)

(Note: Nutritional values are approximate and may vary based on specific ingredients and quantities.)

- Calories: 450
- Protein: 25g
- Fat: 20g
- Carbohydrates: 40g
- Fiber: 2g
- Sugar: 2g
- Sodium: 650mg

MEDITERRANEAN BREAKFAST SANDWICHES

Prep Time: 15 minutes
Cook Time: 10 minutes
Serves: 4

Ingredients:

For the Sandwiches:

- 4 whole-grain English muffins, split and toasted
- 4 large eggs
- 1 cup baby spinach leaves
- 1 large tomato, sliced
- 1/2 cucumber, thinly sliced
- 1/4 cup Kalamata olives, sliced
- 1/4 cup crumbled feta cheese
- Fresh dill for garnish
- Olive oil for cooking

For the Tzatziki Sauce:

- 1/2 cup Greek yogurt
- 1/4 cucumber, finely grated
- 1 clove garlic, minced
- 1 tablespoon fresh lemon juice
- 1 tablespoon fresh dill, chopped
- Salt and pepper to taste

Directions:

1. Prepare Tzatziki Sauce:

- In a bowl, combine Greek yogurt, parsley, minced garlic, grated cucumber, lemon juice, and salt and pepper. Put aside.

2. Cook Eggs:

- In a frying pan, cook olive oil on medium heat. Once the eggs are cracked into the pan, fry them to your preferred consistency (fried or scrambled).

3. Assemble Sandwiches:

- Spread a generous spoonful of tzatziki sauce on each half of a toasted English muffin.
- Top with baby spinach leaves, a slice of tomato, and a few cucumber slices.
- Place the cooked eggs on top of the vegetables.

4. Add Mediterranean Flavors:

- Sprinkle sliced Kalamata olives and crumbled feta cheese over the eggs.
- Garnish with fresh dill.

5. Season and Serve:

- Season the sandwiches with salt and pepper to taste. Place the other half of the toasted English muffin on top.

6. Serve Warm:

- Serve the Mediterranean Breakfast Sandwiches warm and enjoy!

Nutrition Information (per serving):

(Note: Nutritional values are approximate and may vary based on specific ingredients and quantities.)

- Calories: 320
- Protein: 15g
- Fat: 15g
- Carbohydrates: 30g
- Fiber: 6g
- Sugar: 5g
- Sodium: 450mg

BREAKFAST HAM AND EGG CUPS

Prep Time: 10 minutes
Cook Time: 15 minutes
Serves: 6

Ingredients:

- 6 slices of ham
- 6 large eggs
- 1 cup baby spinach, chopped
- 1/2 cup cherry tomatoes, diced
- 1/4 cup shredded cheddar cheese
- Salt and pepper to taste
- Fresh chives for garnish (optional)

Directions:

1. Preheat Oven:
- Set the oven's temperature to 190 degrees Celsius, or 375 degrees Fahrenheit. Put a little bit of cooking spray on a muffin tin.

2. Prepare Ham Cups:
- Put a slice of ham into each muffin cup, shaping it into a cup.

3. Add Vegetables:
- Distribute chopped baby spinach and diced cherry tomatoes evenly among the ham cups.

4. Crack Eggs:
- Crack one egg into each ham cup over the vegetables.

5. Season:
- Add pepper and salt to taste and season each egg.

6. Add Cheese:
- Top each egg with grated cheddar cheese.

7. Bake in the Oven:
- Bake for approximately 15 minutes, or until the yolks are cooked to your preference and the egg whites are set.

8. Garnish and Serve:
- Garnish with fresh chives if desired.

9. Serve Warm:
- Carefully remove the Breakfast Ham and Egg Cups from the muffin tin and serve warm.

Nutrition Information (per serving)

(Note: Nutritional values are approximate and may vary based on specific ingredients and quantities.)

- Calories: 150
- Protein: 15g
- Fat: 9g
- Carbohydrates: 2g
- Fiber: 1g
- Sugar: 1g
- Sodium: 450mg

ASPARAGUS AND PROSCIUTTO FRITTATA

Prep Time: 15 minutes
Cook Time: 20 minutes
Serves: 4

Ingredients:

- 8 large eggs
- 1/2 cup milk
- Salt and pepper to taste
- 1 tablespoon olive oil
- One bunch of asparagus, thinly sliced into 1-inch segments
- 4 slices prosciutto, chopped
- 1/2 cup grated Parmesan cheese
- 1/4 cup fresh chives, chopped
- Cooking spray for the skillet

Directions:

1. Preheat Oven:

- Preheat your oven to 375°F (190°C).

2. Whisk Eggs:

- Whisk together milk, eggs, pepper, and salt until thoroughly mixed.

3. Cook Asparagus and Prosciutto:

- Heat olive oil in an oven-safe skillet over medium heat. Add asparagus pieces and chopped prosciutto. Cook for 3-4 minutes until asparagus is slightly tender.

4. Pour Egg Mixture:

- Transfer the whisked egg mixture onto the prosciutto and cook the asparagus in the skillet.

5. Sprinkle Cheese:

- Sprinkle grated Parmesan cheese evenly over the egg mixture.

6. **Cook on Stovetop:**
    - Cook on the stovetop for 3-4 minutes, allowing the edges to set.

7. **Transfer to Oven:**
    - After transferring the skillet to the oven, bake for 12 to 15 minutes or until the frittata is cooked with a hint of color.

8. **Garnish and Serve:**
    - Take it out of the oven and top it with chopped fresh chives.

9. **Slice and Serve Warm:**
    - Allow the frittata to cool before slicing. Serve warm.

Nutrition Information (per serving)

(Note: Nutritional values are approximate and may vary based on specific ingredients and quantities.)

- Calories: 250
- Protein: 18g
- Fat: 18g
- Carbohydrates: 5g
- Fiber: 2g
- Sugar: 2g
- Sodium: 450mg

GREEK VEGETABLE AND FETA CHEESE PIE (SPANAKOPITA)

Prep Time: 30 minutes
Cook Time: 45 minutes
Serves: 8

Ingredients:

For the Filling:

- 1 tablespoon olive oil
- 1 onion, finely chopped
- 2 garlic cloves, minced
- 1 pound (450g) spinach, washed and chopped
- 1 cup cherry tomatoes, halved
- 1 red bell pepper, diced
- 1 yellow bell pepper, diced
- 1 cup crumbled feta cheese
- 1/4 cup fresh dill, chopped
- Salt and pepper to taste

For the Pastry:

- 10 sheets phyllo dough, thawed if frozen
- 1/2 cup unsalted butter, melted

Directions:

1. Preheat Oven:

- Preheat your oven to 375°F (190°C).

2. Prepare Filling:

- In a large skillet, heat olive oil over medium heat. Add chopped onion and minced garlic. Cook until the onion is translucent.

3. **Cook Vegetables:**
   - Add chopped spinach, cherry tomatoes, diced red and yellow bell peppers to the skillet. Cook until the vegetables are tender and the spinach is wilted. Remove from heat and let it cool.

4. **Mix in Feta and Dill:**
   - Stir in crumbled feta cheese and chopped fresh dill—season with salt and pepper to taste. Allow the filling to cool completely.

5. **Assemble the Pie:**
   - Apply melted butter to a baking dish. Arrange a single phyllo dough sheet in the dish, allowing the sides to overhang. Brush with melted butter. Repeat with additional sheets, layering and buttering each one.

6. **Add Filling:**
   - Spread the cooled vegetable and feta filling evenly over the phyllo layers.

7. **Top with Phyllo:**
   - Place additional phyllo sheets on top, buttering each layer. To make a border, fold the excess edges over the top.

8. **Bake:**
   - Bake in the oven for 40-45 minutes or until the phyllo is golden brown and crispy.

9. **Slice and Serve:**
   - Before slicing, let the pie cool somewhat. Warm up and serve.

Nutrition Information (per serving)

(Note: Nutritional values are approximate and may vary based on specific ingredients and quantities.)

- Calories: 320
- Protein: 10g
- Fat: 22g
- Carbohydrates: 25g
- Fiber: 3g
- Sugar: 3g
- Sodium: 450mg

SPANISH-STYLE TOMATOES ON TOAST

Prep Time: 10 minutes
Cook Time: 5 minutes
Serves: 4

Ingredients:

- 4 large ripe tomatoes, diced
- 2 cloves garlic, minced
- 1/4 cup fresh parsley, chopped
- 2 tablespoons extra-virgin olive oil
- 1 teaspoon red wine vinegar
- Salt and pepper to taste
- 4 slices of rustic bread, toasted
- Optional: 1 teaspoon smoked paprika for garnish

Directions:

1. Prepare Tomatoes:
- Combine the diced tomatoes, minced garlic, chopped parsley, olive oil, red wine vinegar, salt, and pepper in a bowl. Mix well to combine.

2. Let Marinate:
- Allow the tomato mixture to marinate for 10 minutes to melt the flavors.

3. Toast-Bread:
- While the tomatoes are marinating, toast the slices of rustic bread until golden brown.

4. Assemble:
- Spoon the marinated tomato mixture generously over the toasted bread slices.

5. Garnish (Optional):
- If desired, sprinkle a pinch of smoked paprika over each toast for an extra layer of flavor.

6. Serve Immediately:

- Serve the Spanish-style Tomatoes on Toast immediately.

Nutrition Information (per serving)

(Note: Nutritional values are approximate and may vary based on specific ingredients and quantities.)

- Calories: 180
- Protein: 4g
- Fat: 8g
- Carbohydrates: 24g
- Fiber: 3g
- Sugar: 4g
- Sodium: 220mg

OATMEAL WITH YOGURT AND NUTMEG

Prep Time: 5 minutes
Cook Time: 10 minutes
Serves: 2

Ingredients:

- 1 cup old-fashioned oats
- Two cups water or milk (dairy or plant-based)
- 1/2 teaspoon ground nutmeg
- 1/4 teaspoon salt
- 1/2 cup Greek yogurt
- 2 tablespoons honey or maple syrup (optional)
- 1/4 cup chopped nuts, including walnuts and almonds
- Fresh fruit for topping (such as sliced bananas and berries)

Directions:

1. Cook Oats:

- Heat the milk or water in a saucepan until it begins to boil. Add the salt, ground nutmeg, and oats and stir.

2. Simmer:

- Lower heat to medium-low and simmer the oats, occasionally stirring, for about 5-7 minutes or until they reach your desired consistency.

3. Add Yogurt:

- Take the pot off of the burner. Greek yogurt should be added and thoroughly mixed up.

4. Sweeten (Optional):

- If desired, sweeten the oatmeal with honey or maple syrup to taste. Stir until evenly distributed.

5. Serve:

- Divide the oatmeal into serving bowls.

6. Top with Nuts and Fruit:
- Sprinkle chopped nuts over the oatmeal and add fresh fruit on top.

7. Garnish with Nutmeg:
- Grate a little extra nutmeg on top for garnish.

8. Serve Warm:
- Serve the Oatmeal with Yogurt and Nutmeg warm.

Nutrition Information (per serving)

(Note: Nutritional values are approximate and may vary based on specific ingredients and quantities.)

- Calories: 300
- Protein: 12g
- Fat: 8g
- Carbohydrates: 48g
- Fiber: 6g
- Sugar: 10g
- Sodium: 150mg

TURKISH EGGS WITH GREEK YOGURT (CILBIR)

Prep Time: 10 minutes
Cook Time: 5 minutes
Serves: 2

Ingredients:

- 4 large eggs
- 1 cup Greek yogurt
- 2 cloves garlic, minced
- 2 tablespoons extra-virgin olive oil
- 1 teaspoon paprika
- 1/2 teaspoon ground cumin
- Salt and pepper to taste
- Fresh parsley, chopped (for garnish)
- Optional: Red pepper flakes for a spicy kick

Directions:

1. Prepare Yogurt Base:
- Whisk together Greek yogurt, minced garlic, and a pinch of salt in a bowl. Divide the yogurt mixture between two serving plates, creating a smooth egg bed.

2. Poach Eggs:
- Poach the eggs in a saucepan of boiling water until the yolks are still runny, but the whites are set. Usually, this requires three to four minutes. Remove the poached eggs with a slotted spoon and put them over the yogurt.

3. Season with Spices:
- Warm the olive oil over low heat. Add paprika, ground cumin, salt, and pepper. Stir gently until the spices are fragrant. Be careful not to burn them.

4. Drizzle Over Eggs:
- Drizzle the spiced olive oil over the poached eggs and yogurt.

5. Garnish:

- Add freshly cut parsley as a garnish for the Turkish eggs. If the desired level of spice, add red pepper flakes.

6. Serve Immediately:

- Serve the Turkish Eggs with Greek Yogurt immediately, with crusty bread on the side for dipping.

Nutrition Information (per serving)

(Note: Nutritional values are approximate and may vary based on specific ingredients and quantities.)

- Calories: 320
- Protein: 20g
- Fat: 23g
- Carbohydrates: 8g
- Fiber: 1g
- Sugar: 4g
- Sodium: 220mg

THE BEST PROTEIN OATMEAL (WITH QUICK OATS)

Prep Time: 5 minutes
Cook Time: 5 minutes
Serves: 1

Ingredients:

- 1/2 cup quick oats
- 1 cup milk (dairy or plant-based)
- 1 scoop protein powder (flavor of your choice)
- 1 tablespoon chia seeds
- 1 tablespoon nut butter (almond, peanut, or your choice)
- 1 tablespoon honey or maple syrup
- 1/2 teaspoon vanilla extract
- Pinch of salt
- Toppings: Sliced bananas, berries, nuts, seeds

Directions:

1. Cook Oats:
- In a saucepan, combine quick oats and milk. Over medium heat, bring to an average boil, stirring periodically.

2. Add Protein Powder:
- Once the oats start to thicken, reduce the heat to low. After adding the protein powder, whisk everything together well.

3. Incorporate Chia Seeds:
- Add chia seeds to the oat mixture and continue stirring. Let it simmer until the oats are fully cooked, and the mixture reaches your desired consistency.

4. Add Nut Butter and Sweetener:
- Add the vanilla essence, nut butter, honey (or maple syrup), and a small salt. Mix until the nut butter is melted and the oatmeal is well-flavored.

5. Serve:

- Transfer the protein oatmeal to a bowl.

6. Top with Toppings:

- Add your preferred toppings, like chopped bananas, berries, almonds, or sesame seeds, as a garnish.

7. Enjoy Warm:

- Serve The Best Protein Oatmeal warm and enjoy!

Nutrition Information (per serving)

(Note: Nutritional values are approximate and may vary based on specific ingredients and quantities.)

- Calories: 450
- Protein: 25g
- Fat: 15g
- Carbohydrates: 55g
- Fiber: 8g
- Sugar: 20g
- Sodium: 250mg

LABNEH PITA SANDWICH

Prep Time: 10 minutes
Serves: 2

Ingredients:

- 2 large whole wheat pita bread
- 1 cup labneh (strained yogurt)
- 1 cucumber, thinly sliced
- 1 large tomato, sliced
- 1/2 red onion, thinly sliced
- Fresh mint leaves
- Kalamata olives, pitted
- Extra-virgin olive oil
- Salt and pepper to taste

Directions:

1. Prepare Labneh:
- If you haven't already, strain regular yogurt to make labneh by placing it in a cheesecloth-lined strainer over a bowl for a few hours or overnight in the refrigerator.

2. Prepare Vegetables:
- Slice the cucumber, tomato, and red onion thinly.

3. Warm Pita Bread:
- Heat the pita bread briefly in a toaster or grill to make it warm and pliable.

4. Assemble Sandwiches:
- Spread a generous amount of labneh on each pita bread.
- Layer the sliced cucumber, tomato, and red onion on the labneh.

5. Add Fresh Mint and Olives:
- Sprinkle fresh mint leaves over the vegetables and add Kalamata olives.

6. Drizzle with Olive Oil:

- Drizzle extra-virgin olive oil over the assembled sandwich.

7. Season with Salt and Pepper:
- Season with salt and pepper to taste.

8. Fold and Serve:
- Fold the pita in half, creating a sandwich. Repeat for the second sandwich.

9. Serve Immediately:
- Serve the Labneh Pita Sandwiches immediately.

Nutrition Information (per serving)

(Note: Nutritional values are approximate and may vary based on specific ingredients and quantities.)

- Calories: 300
- Protein: 10g
- Fat: 12g
- Carbohydrates: 35g
- Fiber: 6g
- Sugar: 8g
- Sodium: 400mg

Chapter 3: Lunch

PESTO CHICKEN QUINOA BOWLS

Prep Time: 15 minutes
Cook Time: 20 minutes
Serves: 4

Ingredients:

- 1 cup quinoa, rinsed
- 2 cups water or chicken broth
- 4 boneless, skinless chicken breasts
- Salt and pepper to taste
- 1 cup cherry tomatoes, halved
- 1 cup cucumber, diced
- 1/2 cup red bell pepper, diced
- 1/2 cup black olives, sliced
- 1/2 cup feta cheese, crumbled
- Fresh basil leaves for garnish

Pesto Sauce:

- 2 cups fresh basil leaves
- 1/2 cup grated Parmesan cheese
- 1/3 cup pine nuts
- 2 cloves garlic
- 1/2 cup extra-virgin olive oil
- Salt and pepper to taste
- Juice of 1 lemon

Directions:

1. Cook Quinoa:

- In a saucepan, combine quinoa and water or chicken broth. After it boils, reduce the heat, cover it, and simmer it for 15 minutes or until the quinoa is soft and the water has been absorbed.

2. **Season and Cook Chicken:**
   - Season chicken breasts with salt and pepper. In a skillet, heat olive oil over medium heat. Cook until the chicken is cooked, 6 to 8 minutes per side. Before slicing, let it rest for a few minutes.

3. **Prepare Pesto Sauce:**
   - Combine fresh basil, Parmesan cheese, pine nuts, garlic, and lemon juice in a food processor. Pulse until finely chopped. Slowly drizzle the olive oil with the processor until the pesto is smooth—season with salt and pepper to taste.

4. **Assemble Bowls:**
   - In each bowl, layer cooked quinoa, sliced pesto chicken, cherry tomatoes, cucumber, red bell pepper, black olives, and crumbled feta cheese.

5. **Drizzle with Pesto:**
   - Drizzle the pesto sauce over each bowl.

6. **Garnish:**
   - Garnish with fresh basil leaves.

7. **Serve Immediately:**
   - Serve the Pesto Chicken Quinoa Bowls immediately.

Nutrition Information (per serving)

(Note: Nutritional values are approximate and may vary based on specific ingredients and quantities.)

- Calories: 500
- Protein: 30g
- Fat: 28g
- Carbohydrates: 35g
- Fiber: 6g
- Sugar: 4g
- Sodium: 600mg

TOMATO & AVOCADO CHEESE SANDWICH

Prep Time: 10 minutes
Serves: 2

Ingredients:

- 4 slices whole-grain bread
- 1 large tomato, thinly sliced
- 1 ripe avocado, sliced
- 4 slices of your favorite cheese (cheddar, Swiss, or your choice)
- Handful of arugula or spinach leaves
- Salt and pepper to taste
- Olive oil for drizzling (optional)

Directions:

1. Prepare Bread:
- Toast the slices of whole-grain bread to your liking.

2. Layer Cheese:
- Place a slice of cheese on each piece of toasted bread.

3. Add Tomato Slices:
- Layer the tomato slices evenly on top of the cheese.

4. Add Avocado Slices:
- Place the slices of avocado over the tomatoes.

5. Season with Salt and Pepper:
- Season the tomatoes and avocados with a pinch of salt and pepper.

6. Add Greens:
- Place a handful of arugula or spinach leaves on top.

7. Complete the Sandwich:
- Add a second slice of toasted bread on top of each sandwich.

8. Serve:

- When ready to serve, cut the sandwiches in half diagonally.

9. Optional Drizzle:

- If desired, drizzle olive oil over the sandwich for extra flavor.

Nutrition Information (per serving)

(Note: Nutritional values are approximate and may vary based on specific ingredients and quantities.)

- Calories: 400
- Protein: 15g
- Fat: 22g
- Carbohydrates: 40g
- Fiber: 10g
- Sugar: 5g
- Sodium: 400mg

PILED-HIGH VEGETABLE PITAS

Prep Time: 15 minutes
Cook Time: 10 minutes
Serves: 4

Ingredients:

For the Tzatziki Sauce:

- 1 cup Greek yogurt
- 1 cucumber, peeled, seeded, and finely chopped
- 2 cloves garlic, minced
- 1 tablespoon fresh dill, chopped
- 1 tablespoon extra-virgin olive oil
- Salt and pepper to taste

For the Vegetable Filling:

- 1 cup cherry tomatoes, halved
- 1 cucumber, sliced
- 1 red bell pepper, thinly sliced
- 1 red onion, thinly sliced
- 1 cup shredded lettuce or spinach
- 1/2 cup Kalamata olives, sliced
- 4 whole-grain pita bread rounds

Optional Protein (Choose One):

- Grilled chicken strips
- Falafel balls
- Chickpeas (roasted or boiled)

Directions:

1. Combine Greek yogurt, chopped cucumber, minced garlic, chopped fresh dill, and olive oil in a bowl.

2. Season with salt and pepper to taste.
3. Mix well and refrigerate while preparing the rest of the ingredients.

For the Vegetable Filling:

1. Combine cherry tomatoes, sliced cucumber, red bell pepper, red onion, shredded lettuce or spinach, and Kalamata olives in a large bowl.
2. Toss the vegetables until well mixed.

Assembly:

1. Toasted or grilled pita bread rounds can be warmed.
2. Distribute a substantial quantity of tzatziki sauce into every pita pocket.
3. Fill each pita pocket with the mixed vegetables.
4. Add your choice of protein: grilled chicken strips, falafel balls, or chickpeas.
5. Serve immediately.

Nutrition Information (per serving)

(Note: Nutritional values are approximate and may vary based on specific ingredients and quantities.)

- Calories: 350 (without protein)
- Protein: 10g (varies with protein choice)
- Fat: 8g
- Carbohydrates: 60g
- Fiber: 8g
- Sugar: 10g
- Sodium: 500mg

CUCUMBER-CHICKEN GREEN GODDESS WRAP

Prep Time: 15 minutes
Cook Time: 10 minutes (if cooking chicken)
Serves: 2

Ingredients:

For the Green Goddess Dressing:

- 1/2 cup Greek yogurt
- 1/4 cup fresh basil leaves
- 1/4 cup fresh parsley leaves
- 1 tablespoon lemon juice
- 1 clove garlic
- Salt and pepper to taste

For the Wrap:

- 2 large whole-grain wraps or tortillas
- One cup of cooked, sliced, or shredded chicken breast
- 1 cucumber, thinly sliced
- 1 avocado, sliced
- 1 cup mixed greens (arugula, spinach, or your choice)
- 1/2 cup cherry tomatoes, halved
- Optional: Feta cheese crumbles

Directions:

For the Green Goddess Dressing:

1. Add the Greek yogurt, garlic, lemon juice, parsley, and basil leaves to a food processor or blender.
2. Blend until smooth.
3. Season with salt and pepper to taste. Set aside.

For the Wrap:

1. If not using pre-cooked chicken, cook the chicken breast until fully cooked—season with salt and pepper.
2. Spread a generous amount of the Green Goddess Dressing in each whole-grain wrap.
3. Layer with cooked chicken, cucumber, avocado, mixed greens, and cherry tomatoes.
4. Optional: Sprinkle with feta cheese crumbles for added flavor.
5. Tightly roll the wrap by folding it in the sides.
6. Cut in half diagonally and secure with toothpicks if needed.
7. Serve immediately and enjoy!

Nutrition Information (per serving)

(Note: Nutritional values are approximate and may vary based on specific ingredients and quantities.)

- Calories: 400
- Protein: 25g
- Fat: 18g
- Carbohydrates: 35g
- Fiber: 10g
- Sugar: 5g
- Sodium: 600mg

MEDITERRANEAN PASTA SALAD

Prep Time: 15 minutes
Cook Time: 10 minutes (for pasta)
Serves: 4

Ingredients:

For the Salad:

- 8 oz (about 2 cups) rotini or fusilli pasta, cooked and cooled
- 1 cup cherry tomatoes, halved
- 1 cucumber, diced
- 1/2 red bell pepper, diced
- 1/2 red onion, finely chopped
- 1/2 cup Kalamata olives, sliced
- 1/2 cup feta cheese, crumbled
- 1/4 cup fresh parsley, chopped

For the Dressing:

- 1/4 cup extra-virgin olive oil
- 2 tablespoons red wine vinegar
- 1 clove garlic, minced
- 1 teaspoon dried oregano
- Salt and pepper to taste

Directions:

1. Make the pasta. Empty, give a quick rinse with cold water, and leave to cool.
2. Combine the cooled pasta, cherry tomatoes, cucumber, red bell pepper, red onion, Kalamata olives, feta cheese, and fresh parsley in a large bowl.
3. To create the dressing, in a small basin or container, whisk together the olive oil, red wine vinegar, minced garlic, dried oregano, salt, and pepper.
4. Cover the pasta and veggies with the dressing. Toss lightly to coat all items equally.
5. Taste and adjust the seasoning if needed.

6. To allow the flavors to meld, let the pasta salad sit in the refrigerator for at least 30 minutes before serving.
7. Serve cold, and enjoy!

Nutrition Information (per serving)

(Note: Nutritional values are approximate and may vary based on specific ingredients and quantities.)

- Calories: 350
- Protein: 8g
- Fat: 18g
- Carbohydrates: 40g
- Fiber: 4g
- Sugar: 4g
- Sodium: 450mg

VEGETARIAN PROTEIN BOWL

Prep Time: 15 minutes
Cook Time: 15 minutes
Serves: 2

Ingredients:

For the Bowl:

- 1 cup quinoa, rinsed
- 2 cups water or vegetable broth
- 1 cup canned chickpeas, drained and rinsed
- 1 cup cherry tomatoes, halved
- 1 cucumber, diced
- 1/2 cup red onion, finely chopped
- 1/2 cup feta cheese, crumbled
- 1/4 cup Kalamata olives, sliced
- Fresh parsley for garnish

For the Tahini Dressing:

- 1/4 cup tahini
- 2 tablespoons lemon juice
- 1 tablespoon olive oil
- 1 clove garlic, minced
- Salt and pepper to taste
- Water (to thin as needed)

Directions:

1. For the Quinoa:

- In a saucepan, combine quinoa and water or vegetable broth. After heating to a boil, reduce heat, cover, and simmer for 14-15 minutes or until the quinoa is firm and the water has been completely absorbed.
- Once the quinoa is fluffy, leave it aside.

2. For the Tahini Dressing:

- In a tiny bowl, whisk together the tahini, lemon juice, olive oil, minced garlic, salt, and pepper.
- Add water gradually until the dressing reaches your desired consistency. Set aside.

3. Assembling the Bowl:

- Layer cooked quinoa, chickpeas, cherry tomatoes, cucumber, red onion, feta cheese, and Kalamata olives in each bowl.
- Drizzle the tahini dressing over the bowl.
- Garnish with fresh parsley.
- Toss gently to combine all the ingredients.
- Serve and enjoy!

Nutrition Information (per serving)

(Note: Nutritional values are approximate and may vary based on specific ingredients and quantities.)

- Calories: 450
- Protein: 15g
- Fat: 20g
- Carbohydrates: 55g
- Fiber: 10g
- Sugar: 4g
- Sodium: 600mg

ROASTED SALMON RICE BOWL WITH BEETS & BRUSSELS

Prep Time: 15 minutes
Cook Time: 25 minutes
Serves: 2

Ingredients:

For the Salmon:

- 2 salmon fillets (about 6 oz each)
- 1 tablespoon olive oil
- 1 teaspoon lemon juice
- Salt and pepper to taste

For the Vegetables:

- 1 cup Brussels sprouts, halved
- 1 cup beets, peeled and diced
- 2 tablespoons olive oil
- Salt and pepper to taste

For the Rice:

- 1 cup brown rice, cooked

For the Avocado Yogurt Sauce:

- 1 ripe avocado, mashed
- 1/2 cup Greek yogurt
- 1 tablespoon lemon juice
- Salt and pepper to taste

Directions:

1. For the Salmon:
- Preheat the oven to 400°F (200°C).
- Place salmon fillets on a baking sheet. Drizzle with olive oil, lemon juice, salt, and pepper.
- Roast in the oven for 15-20 minutes or until the salmon is cooked and flakes easily with a fork.

2. For the Vegetables:
- Toss Brussels sprouts and diced beets with olive oil, salt, and pepper in a bowl.
- Arrange the veggies on a different baking sheet.
- Roast in the oven for about 20-25 minutes or until the vegetables are tender and slightly caramelized.

3. For the Avocado Yogurt Sauce:
- Combine mashed avocado, Greek yogurt, lemon juice, salt, and pepper in a small bowl. Mix well.

4. Assembly:
- In serving bowls, layer cooked brown rice, Brussels sprouts, beets, and a roasted salmon fillet.
- Drizzle with avocado yogurt sauce.
- Serve immediately and enjoy!

Nutrition Information (per serving)

(Note: Nutritional values are approximate and may vary based on specific ingredients and quantities.)

- Calories: 550
- Protein: 30g
- Fat: 30g
- Carbohydrates: 40g
- Fiber: 9g
- Sugar: 4g
- Sodium: 300mg

MEDITERRANEAN VEGETABLE SOUP

Prep Time: 15 minutes
Cook Time: 30 minutes
Serves: 4

Ingredients:

- 2 tablespoons olive oil
- 1 onion, finely chopped
- 2 carrots, diced
- 2 celery stalks, diced
- 3 cloves garlic, minced
- 1 zucchini, diced
- 1 yellow bell pepper, diced
- 1 red bell pepper, diced
- 1 can (14 oz) diced tomatoes, undrained
- 4 cups vegetable broth
- 1 teaspoon dried oregano
- 1 teaspoon dried basil
- 1/2 teaspoon dried thyme
- Salt and pepper to taste
- 1 cup cooked chickpeas (canned or cooked from dried)
- 1 cup spinach leaves, chopped
- Juice of 1 lemon
- Fresh parsley for garnish

Directions:

1. Warm up the olive oil in a big pot over medium heat. Add chopped onion, carrots, and celery. Sauté until vegetables are softened, about 5 minutes.
2. Add minced garlic and sauté for an additional minute until fragrant.
3. Add diced zucchini, yellow bell pepper, and red bell pepper. Cook for another 5 minutes, stirring occasionally.

4. Pour in diced tomatoes with their juice, vegetable broth, dried oregano, dried basil, dried thyme, salt, and pepper. Bring the soup to a simmer.
5. Reduce heat to low, cover, and let the soup simmer for 15-20 minutes to allow the flavors to meld.
6. Add cooked chickpeas and chopped spinach. Stir well and let it simmer for 5 minutes until the spinach is wilted.
7. Squeeze in the juice from one lemon and mix the soup just before serving.
8. Taste and adjust the seasoning if needed.
9. Serve hot, garnished with fresh parsley.

Nutrition Information (per serving)

(Note: Nutritional values are approximate and may vary based on specific ingredients and quantities.)

- Calories: 200
- Protein: 6g
- Fat: 6g
- Carbohydrates: 32g
- Fiber: 8g
- Sugar: 10g
- Sodium: 800mg

3-INGREDIENT ROASTED RED PEPPER SOUP WITH CHICKPEAS

Prep Time: 5 minutes
Cook Time: 20 minutes
Serves: 4

Ingredients:

- 2 jars (about 24 oz) roasted red peppers, drained
- one can (14 oz) chickpeas, drained and rinsed
- 4 cups vegetable broth
- Salt and pepper to taste
- Optional toppings: Greek yogurt, fresh parsley, or a drizzle of olive oil

Directions:

1. In a blender, combine the roasted red peppers and chickpeas.
2. Add vegetable broth to the blender.
3. Blend the mixture until it's well incorporated and smooth.
4. Transfer the blend to a pot and let it warm over medium flame.
5. Season with salt and pepper to taste.
6. Bring the soup to a simmer and let it cook for about 15-20 minutes, stirring occasionally.
7. Taste and adjust the seasoning if needed.
8. Serve hot, optionally topped with a dollop of Greek yogurt, fresh parsley, or a drizzle of olive oil.

Nutrition Information (per serving)

(Note: Nutritional values are approximate and may vary based on specific ingredients and quantities.)

- Calories: 150
- Protein: 6g
- Fat: 2g

- Carbohydrates: 29g
- Fiber: 6g
- Sugar: 6g
- Sodium: 800mg

CHICKEN & CUCUMBER PITA SANDWICHES WITH YOGURT SAUCE

Prep Time: 15 minutes
Cook Time: 15 minutes
Serves: 4

Ingredients:

For the Chicken:

- One pound of finely sliced, boneless, skinless chicken breasts
- 2 tablespoons olive oil
- 1 teaspoon ground cumin
- 1 teaspoon smoked paprika
- Salt and pepper to taste

For the Yogurt Sauce:

- 1 cup Greek yogurt
- One cucumber, grated and squeezed to remove excess moisture
- 2 cloves garlic, minced
- 1 tablespoon fresh dill, chopped
- Salt and pepper to taste

For the Sandwiches:

- Four half-cut whole-wheat pita breads
- 1 cucumber, thinly sliced
- 1 cup cherry tomatoes, halved

- 1 red onion, thinly sliced
- Fresh lettuce leaves

Directions:

1. For the Chicken:
- Combine sliced chicken, olive oil, ground cumin, smoked paprika, salt, and pepper in a bowl. Toss to coat the chicken evenly.
- In a skillet, preheat the heat to medium-high. After adding the seasoning, cook the chicken for 6 to 8 minutes or until it is done.

2. For the Yogurt Sauce:
- Mix Greek yogurt, grated cucumber, minced garlic, fresh dill, salt, and pepper in a bowl. Stir until well combined.

3. Assembly:
- Preheat the pita bread in the oven or skillet for a brief while.
- Fill each half of a pita with a large quantity of the yogurt sauce.
- Fill each pita with cooked chicken, cucumber slices, cherry tomatoes, red onion, and fresh lettuce.
- Drizzle with extra yogurt sauce if desired.
- Serve immediately and enjoy!

Nutrition Information (per serving)

(Note: Nutritional values are approximate and may vary based on specific ingredients and quantities.)

- Calories: 400
- Protein: 30g
- Fat: 12g
- Carbohydrates: 45g
- Fiber: 8g
- Sugar: 8g
- Sodium: 450mg

SLOW-COOKER CHICKEN & CHICKPEA SOUP

Prep Time: 15 minutes
Cook Time: 4-6 hours (on low) or 2-3 hours (on high)
Serves: 6-8

Ingredients:

- 1.5 pounds boneless, skinless chicken thighs
- One can (15 oz) chickpeas, drained and rinsed
- 1 cup carrots, diced
- 1 cup celery, diced
- 1 onion, finely chopped
- 3 cloves garlic, minced
- 1 can (14 oz) diced tomatoes, undrained
- 6 cups chicken broth
- 1 teaspoon dried thyme
- 1 teaspoon dried rosemary
- Salt and pepper to taste
- 2 cups spinach leaves, chopped
- Fresh parsley for garnish

Directions:

1. Set the chicken thighs in the slow cooker, starting at the bottom.
2. Add chickpeas, carrots, celery, onion, and garlic to the slow cooker.
3. Pour diced tomatoes (with their juice) and chicken broth over the ingredients.
4. Season with dried thyme, dried rosemary, salt, and pepper. Stir to combine.
5. Once the chicken is cooked, cover and simmer on low for 4-6 hours or on high for 2-3 hours.
6. About 30 minutes before serving, shred the chicken using two forks and return it to the slow cooker.
7. Add the chopped spinach and heat, stirring, until it wilts.
8. Taste and adjust the seasoning if needed.
9. Serve hot, garnished with fresh parsley.

Nutrition Information (per serving)

(Note: Nutritional values are approximate and may vary based on specific ingredients and quantities.)

- Calories: 250
- Protein: 25g
- Fat: 6g
- Carbohydrates: 25g
- Fiber: 6g
- Sugar: 6g
- Sodium: 800mg

PROSCIUTTO, MOZZARELLA & MELON PLATE

Prep Time: 15 minutes
Cook Time: 0 minutes
Serves: 4

Ingredients:

- 8 slices prosciutto
- 1 medium-sized melon (cantaloupe or honeydew), peeled, seeded, and sliced
- 8 ounces fresh mozzarella, sliced
- Balsamic glaze (optional)
- Fresh basil leaves for garnish

Directions:

1. Arrange the slices of prosciutto on a serving platter.
2. Place melon and fresh mozzarella slices alternately on the platter, creating an attractive pattern.
3. If desired, drizzle balsamic glaze over the melon and mozzarella.
4. Garnish with fresh basil leaves.
5. Enjoy the delightful combination of flavors!

Nutrition Information (per serving)

(Note: Nutritional values are approximate and may vary based on specific ingredients and quantities.)

- Calories: 180
- Protein: 12g
- Fat: 10g
- Carbohydrates: 14g
- Fiber: 1g
- Sugar: 12g
- Sodium: 600mg

RAVIOLI & VEGETABLE SOUP

Prep Time: 15 minutes
Cook Time: 25 minutes
Serves: 6

Ingredients:

- 1 tablespoon olive oil
- 1 onion, finely chopped
- 2 carrots, diced
- 2 celery stalks, diced
- 3 cloves garlic, minced
- 6 cups vegetable broth
- 1 can (14 oz) diced tomatoes, undrained
- 1 teaspoon dried oregano
- 1 teaspoon dried basil
- Salt and pepper to taste
- 1 zucchini, diced
- 1 cup frozen peas
- 1 package (about 20 oz) refrigerated cheese ravioli
- Fresh basil leaves for garnish
- Grated Parmesan cheese for serving

Directions:

1. Warm up the olive oil in a big pot over medium heat. Add chopped onion, carrots, and celery. Sauté until vegetables are softened, about 5 minutes.
2. Add minced garlic and sauté for an additional minute until fragrant.
3. Add the chopped tomatoes and the vegetable broth. Add the salt, pepper, dried basil, and oregano. Simmer the soup for a while.
4. Add diced zucchini and frozen peas. Let the soup simmer for about 10 minutes until the vegetables are tender.
5. Meanwhile, prepare the cheese ravioli as directed on the package. After draining, set away.

6. Add the cooked ravioli to the broth after the vegetables are soft. Gently stir.
7. Taste and adjust the seasoning if needed.
8. Sprinkle with freshly chopped basil leaves and serve hot, dusted with grated Parmesan cheese.

Nutrition Information (per serving)

(Note: Nutritional values are approximate and may vary based on specific ingredients and quantities.)

- Calories: 350
- Protein: 15g
- Fat: 8g
- Carbohydrates: 55g
- Fiber: 7g
- Sugar: 8g
- Sodium: 900mg

TUNA & OLIVE SPINACH SALAD

Prep Time: 10 minutes
Cook Time: 0 minutes
Serves: 2

Ingredients:

- 2 cans (5 oz each) tuna, drained
- 4 cups fresh baby spinach leaves
- 1 cup cherry tomatoes, halved
- 1/2 cup pitted and sliced Kalamata olives
- 1/4 red onion, thinly sliced
- 1/4 cup feta cheese, crumbled
- 2 tablespoons extra-virgin olive oil
- 1 tablespoon red wine vinegar
- 1 teaspoon Dijon mustard
- Salt and pepper to taste
- Fresh lemon wedges for serving (optional)

Directions:

1. Mix fresh baby spinach, cherry tomatoes, Kalamata olives, and thinly sliced red onion in a large salad dish.
2. Add drained tuna to the salad.
3. Whisk together the extra virgin olive oil, red wine vinegar, Dijon mustard, salt, and pepper for the dressing.
4. Pour the salad dressing over it and gently mix to coat all ingredients.
5. Sprinkle crumbled feta cheese over the top.
6. Serve the Tuna & Olive Spinach Salad on plates.
7. Optionally, serve with fresh lemon wedges for a burst of citrus flavor.

Nutrition Information (per serving)

(Note: Nutritional values are approximate and may vary based on specific ingredients and quantities.)

- Calories: 400
- Protein: 30g
- Fat: 20g
- Carbohydrates: 20g
- Fiber: 7g
- Sugar: 5g
- Sodium: 900mg

MEAL-PREP ROASTED VEGETABLE BOWLS WITH PESTO

Prep Time: 15 minutes
Cook Time: 25 minutes
Serves: 4

Ingredients:

For the Roasted Vegetables:

- 2 cups broccoli florets
- 1 bell pepper, sliced
- 1 zucchini, sliced
- 1 yellow squash, sliced
- 1 red onion, sliced
- 2 tablespoons olive oil
- Salt and pepper to taste
- 1 teaspoon dried Italian herbs (optional)

For the Pesto:

- 2 cups fresh basil leaves
- 1/2 cup grated Parmesan cheese
- 1/2 cup pine nuts or walnuts
- 2 cloves garlic, minced
- 1/2 cup extra-virgin olive oil
- Salt and pepper to taste
- Juice of 1 lemon

For Assembly:

- 2 cups cooked quinoa or your choice of grain
- 1 cup cherry tomatoes, halved
- 1/2 cup feta cheese, crumbled (optional)
- Fresh basil leaves for garnish

Directions:

1. Roasted Vegetables:

- Preheat the oven to 425°F (220°C).
- Toss broccoli florets, bell pepper slices, zucchini, yellow squash, red onion with olive oil, salt, pepper, and dried Italian herbs in a large bowl.
- Arrange the vegetables in a single layer on a baking sheet.
- Roast the vegetables in the oven for 21 to 25 minutes, stirring occasionally, or until they are soft and beginning to caramelize.

2. Pesto:

- Combine fresh basil, grated Parmesan cheese, pine nuts or walnuts, minced garlic, olive oil, salt, pepper, and lemon juice in a food processor.
- Blend until smooth and well combined.

3. Assembly:

- Divide the cooked quinoa among four meal-prep containers.
- Top each container with a portion of the roasted vegetables.
- Add cherry tomatoes and crumbled feta cheese (if using).
- Drizzle a generous spoonful of pesto over each bowl.
- Garnish with fresh basil leaves.
- When you're ready to eat, seal the containers and keep them chilled.

Nutrition Information (per serving)

(Note: Nutritional values are approximate and may vary based on specific ingredients and quantities.)

- Calories: 500
- Protein: 12g
- Fat: 35g
- Carbohydrates: 40g
- Fiber: 8g
- Sugar: 6g
- Sodium: 300mg

GREEK CHICKEN AND RICE SKILLET

Prep Time: 15 minutes
Cook Time: 25 minutes
Serves: 4

Ingredients:

- One and a half pounds of skinless, boneless chicken thighs sliced into small pieces
- 1 cup jasmine rice, uncooked
- 1 red bell pepper, diced
- 1 yellow bell pepper, diced
- 1 red onion, finely chopped
- 3 cloves garlic, minced
- 1 cup cherry tomatoes, halved
- 1/2 cup pitted and sliced Kalamata olives
- 1/4 cup feta cheese, crumbled
- 2 tablespoons olive oil
- 1 teaspoon dried oregano
- 1 teaspoon dried thyme
- Salt and pepper to taste
- Fresh parsley for garnish

Directions:

1. Heat the olive oil in a big skillet over medium-high heat.
2. Cook the chicken pieces in the skillet for 5 to 7 minutes or until they are browned all over.
3. Take the chicken out and place it aside from the skillet.
4. Add chopped red and yellow bell peppers, diced red onion, and minced garlic in the same skillet. Sauté until the vegetables are softened, about 5 minutes.
5. Add the uncooked jasmine rice, salt, pepper, dried thyme, and oregano. Toss the rice and cook for a further two minutes.
6. Add the browned chicken, cherry tomatoes, and sliced Kalamata olives to the skillet. Mix well.

7. After adding two cups of water to the skillet, cook the mixture.
8. After the rice and chicken are tender, reduce the heat to a simmer for 16 to 20 minutes, cover the skillet, and cook.
9. After the rice is done, use a fork to fluff it and taste it for flavor. As necessary, adjust the salt and pepper.
10. Add some chopped feta cheese over top and some fresh parsley as a garnish.
11. Serve the Greek Chicken and Rice Skillet hot, and enjoy!

Nutrition Information (per serving):

- Calories: 450
- Protein: 30g
- Fat: 18g
- Carbohydrates: 40g
- Fiber: 4g
- Sugar: 5g
- Sodium: 600mg

MINI CHICKEN SHAWARMA

Prep Time: 20 minutes
Marination Time: 1-2 hours (optional)
Cook Time: 15 minutes
Serves: 4

Ingredients:

For the Marinade:

- One pound of finely sliced, skinless, boneless chicken thighs
- 3 tablespoons plain yogurt
- 2 tablespoons olive oil
- 2 cloves garlic, minced
- 1 teaspoon ground cumin
- 1 teaspoon ground coriander
- 1 teaspoon ground paprika
- 1 teaspoon ground turmeric
- 1 teaspoon ground cinnamon
- 1 teaspoon ground cayenne pepper (adjust to taste)
- Salt and pepper to taste

For the Garlic Sauce:

- 1/2 cup plain yogurt
- 2 cloves garlic, minced
- 1 tablespoon lemon juice
- Salt to taste

For Serving:

- Mini pita bread or flatbreads
- Sliced cucumbers
- Cherry tomatoes, halved
- Red onion, thinly sliced
- Fresh parsley, chopped

Directions:

1. In a bowl, mix all the marinade ingredients: yogurt, olive oil, minced garlic, ground cumin, ground coriander, ground paprika, ground turmeric, ground cinnamon, ground cayenne pepper, salt, and pepper.
2. Add the thinly sliced chicken thighs to the marinade, ensuring they are well-coated. Cover and refrigerate for at least 1-2 hours (marination is optional but enhances flavor).
3. Preheat the oven to 400°F (200°C).
4. Thread the marinated chicken slices onto skewers.
5. After the chicken has cooked and browned slightly, place the skewers on a baking sheet covered with parchment paper and bake for 15 minutes.
6. Prepare the garlic sauce. Mix yogurt, minced garlic, lemon juice, and salt in a bowl. Adjust the seasoning to taste.
7. Once the chicken is done, remove it from the oven and rest for a few minutes.
8. Warm the mini pita bread or flatbreads.
9. Serve the Mini Chicken Shawarma by placing the chicken on the warm bread and topping it with sliced cucumbers, cherry tomatoes, red onion, chopped parsley, and a drizzle of garlic sauce.

Nutrition Information (per serving, excluding bread)

(Note: Nutritional values are approximate and may vary based on specific ingredients and quantities.)

- Calories: 250
- Protein: 25g
- Fat: 12g
- Carbohydrates: 10g
- Fiber: 2g
- Sugar: 4g
- Sodium: 300mg

15-MINUTE MEDITERRANEAN COUSCOUS WITH TUNA AND PEPPERONCINI

Prep Time: 5 minutes
Cook Time: 10 minutes
Serves: 4

Ingredients:

- 1 cup couscous
- 1 can (5 oz) tuna, drained
- 1/2 cup Kalamata olives, sliced
- 1/4 cup pepperoncini, chopped
- 1/4 cup feta cheese, crumbled
- 2 tablespoons extra-virgin olive oil
- 1 tablespoon red wine vinegar
- 1 teaspoon dried oregano
- Salt and pepper to taste
- Fresh parsley for garnish (optional)
- Lemon wedges for serving

Directions:

1. Bring 1 1/4 cups of water to a boil in a medium saucepan.
2. Stir in the couscous, cover the saucepan, and remove it from heat. To give the couscous time to absorb the water, let it sit for five minutes.
3. Separate the grains in the couscous by fluffing it with a fork.
4. Combine the cooked couscous, drained tuna, sliced Kalamata olives, chopped pepperoncini, and crumbled feta cheese in a large bowl.
5. Mix the red wine vinegar, dried oregano, virgin, salt, pepper, and olive oil in a bowl.
6. Pour the dressing over the couscous combination and stir everything thoroughly.
7. Garnish with fresh parsley if desired.
8. Serve the Mediterranean Couscous with Tuna and Pepperoncini in bowls, and add lemon wedges on the side for extra flavor.

Nutrition Information (per serving):

- Calories: 300
- Protein: 15g
- Fat: 12g
- Carbohydrates: 35g
- Fiber: 4g
- Sugar: 1g
- Sodium: 600mg

PESTO QUINOA BOWLS WITH ROASTED VEGGIES AND LABNEH

Prep Time: 15 minutes
Cook Time: 25 minutes
Serves: 4

Ingredients:

For the Pesto Quinoa:

- 1 cup quinoa, rinsed
- 2 cups water
- 1/4 cup pesto sauce (store-bought or homemade)

For the Roasted Veggies:

- 2 cups cherry tomatoes, halved
- 1 large zucchini, sliced
- 1 red bell pepper, sliced
- 1 red onion, sliced
- 2 tablespoons olive oil
- Salt and pepper to taste

For Assembly:

- Labneh (strained yogurt)
- Fresh basil leaves for garnish

Directions:

1. Preparing the Pesto Quinoa:

- Quinoa and water should be combined in a medium pot. After bringing it to a boil, lower the heat to a simmer, cover, and cook the quinoa for fifteen minutes or until the water has been absorbed.
- Fluff the quinoa with a fork and stir in the pesto sauce. Set aside.

2. Roasting the Veggies:

- Preheat the oven to 400°F (200°C).
- In a sizable mixing basin, toss the sliced zucchini, red bell pepper, red onion, and half of the cherry tomatoes with olive oil; season with salt and pepper.
- Spread the veggies in a single layer on a baking sheet.
- Bake the vegetables for 20 to 25 minutes or until they are soft and have started to caramelize.

3. Assembly:

- Divide the pesto quinoa among serving bowls.
- Top the quinoa with the roasted veggies.
- Spoon labneh over the veggies.
- Garnish with fresh basil leaves.
- Drizzle with extra pesto sauce if desired.

Nutrition Information (per serving):

- Calories: 400
- Protein: 12g
- Fat: 18g
- Carbohydrates: 50g
- Fiber: 7g
- Sugar: 6g
- Sodium: 300mg

15-MINUTE MEZZE PLATE WITH TOASTED ZA'ATAR PITA BREAD

Prep Time: 10 minutes
Cook Time: 5 minutes
Serves: 4

Ingredients:

For the Mezze Plate:

- Hummus (store-bought or homemade)
- Tzatziki sauce
- Kalamata olives
- Cherry tomatoes, halved
- Cucumber, sliced
- Feta cheese, crumbled
- Fresh mint leaves
- Extra-virgin olive oil for drizzling
- Lemon wedges for serving

For the Toasted Za'atar Pita Bread:

- 4 whole wheat pita bread
- 2 tablespoons olive oil
- 1 tablespoon za'atar spice blend

Directions:

1. Toasted Za'atar Pita Bread:

- Preheat the oven to 400°F (200°C).
- Brush each pita bread with olive oil on both sides.
- Sprinkle za'atar spice blend evenly over each pita.
- Arrange the ready pitas onto a baking sheet and bake for approximately 5 minutes or until they turn golden and crisp.
- Remove from the oven and let them cool for a few minutes.

2. Assembling the Mezze Plate:

1. Arrange the hummus, tzatziki sauce, Kalamata olives, cherry tomatoes, sliced cucumber, and crumbled feta on a serving platter.
2. Place the toasted za'atar pita bread alongside the mezze ingredients.
3. Drizzle extra-virgin olive oil over the hummus and sprinkle fresh mint leaves.
4. Serve the mezze plate with lemon wedges on the side.

Nutrition Information (per serving):

- Calories: 300
- Protein: 8g
- Fat: 15g
- Carbohydrates: 35g
- Fiber: 6g
- Sugar: 3g
- Sodium: 400mg

Chapter 4: Dinner

WALNUT-ROSEMARY CRUSTED SALMON

Prep Time: 10 minutes
Cook Time: 15 minutes
Serves: 4

Ingredients:

- 4 salmon fillets (about 6 oz each)
- 1 cup walnuts, finely chopped
- 2 tablespoons fresh rosemary, chopped
- 2 tablespoons Dijon mustard
- 1 tablespoon honey
- 1 tablespoon olive oil
- Salt and black pepper to taste
- Lemon wedges for serving
- Fresh rosemary sprigs for garnish (optional)

Directions:

1. Preheat the oven to 400°F (200°C). Line a baking sheet with parchment paper.
2. Mix the finely chopped walnuts and chopped fresh rosemary in a bowl.
3. Separately, whisk together the honey, olive oil, and Dijon mustard.
4. Use salt and black pepper for seasoning the salmon fillets.
5. Brush the mustard-honey mixture over the top of each salmon fillet.
6. Press the walnut-rosemary mixture onto the mustard-coated side of each salmon fillet, ensuring an even coating.
7. Arrange the coated salmon fillets onto the ready baking sheet.
8. Bake in the oven for about 12-15 minutes or until the salmon is cooked and the walnut crust is golden brown.
9. Take it out of the oven and give it some time to rest.
10. Serve the walnut-rosemary-crusted salmon with lemon wedges on top, if desired, and garnish with fresh rosemary sprigs.

Nutrition Information (per serving):

- Calories: 400
- Protein: 30g
- Fat: 28g
- Carbohydrates: 10g
- Fiber: 3g
- Sugar: 4g
- Sodium: 300mg

CHARRED SHRIMP, PESTO & QUINOA BOWLS

Prep Time: 15 minutes
Cook Time: 10 minutes
Serves: 4

Ingredients:

For the Shrimp:

- 1 pound large shrimp, peeled and deveined
- 2 tablespoons olive oil
- 1 teaspoon smoked paprika
- Salt and black pepper to taste
- Lemon wedges for serving

For the Pesto Quinoa:

- 1 cup quinoa, rinsed
- 2 cups water
- 1/2 cup pesto sauce (store-bought or homemade)

For Assembly:

- Cherry tomatoes, halved
- Avocado, sliced
- Fresh basil leaves for garnish
- Pine nuts for garnish (optional)

Directions:

1. Charred Shrimp:

- Toss the shrimp with olive oil, smoked paprika, salt, and black pepper in a bowl.
- Heat a skillet or grill pan over medium-high heat. Add them and fry on each side for two to three minutes when the shrimp are blackened and cooked.
- Squeeze lemon juice over the shrimp and set aside.

2. **Pesto Quinoa:**
   - Quinoa and water should be combined in a medium pot. Lower the heat to a simmer when it comes to a boil, then cover and let the quinoa cook for fifteen minutes or until all of the water is absorbed.
   - Using a fork, fluff the quinoa and then toss in the pesto sauce.

3. **Assembly:**
   - Divide the pesto quinoa among serving bowls.
   - Top with charred shrimp, halved cherry tomatoes, and sliced avocado.
   - If preferred, garnish with pine nuts and fresh basil leaves.
   - Serve it with lemon wedges on the side.

Nutrition Information (per serving)

(Note: Nutritional values are approximate and may vary based on specific ingredients and quantities.)

- Calories: 450
- Protein: 25g
- Fat: 22g
- Carbohydrates: 40g
- Fiber: 7g
- Sugar: 2g
- Sodium: 300mg

SHEET-PAN SALMON WITH SWEET POTATOES & BROCCOLI

Prep Time: 15 minutes
Cook Time: 20 minutes
Serves: 4

Ingredients:

- 4 salmon fillets (about 6 oz each)
- 2 medium sweet potatoes, peeled and diced
- 1 broccoli crown, cut into florets
- 3 tablespoons olive oil
- 2 tablespoons Dijon mustard
- 2 tablespoons maple syrup
- 1 teaspoon garlic powder
- Salt and black pepper to taste
- Lemon wedges for serving

Directions:

1. Set the oven's temperature to 400°F or 200°C. Put parchment paper on the bottom of a large baking sheet.
2. In a bowl, whisk together olive oil, Dijon mustard, maple syrup, salt, black pepper, and garlic powder.
3. Place the diced sweet potatoes and broccoli florets on the prepared baking sheet.
4. Drizzle half of the mustard-maple mixture over the vegetables and toss to coat.
5. Push the vegetables to the sides of the baking sheet to create space for the salmon fillets.
6. Place the salmon fillets in the center of the sheet. Brush the remaining mustard-maple mixture over the salmon.
7. Bake for around 20 minutes, stirring regularly, or until the vegetables are tender and the fish is done.
8. Remove from the oven and serve the Sheet-Pan Salmon with Sweet Potatoes & Broccoli immediately with lemon wedges.

Nutrition Information (per serving)

(Note: Nutritional values are approximate and may vary based on specific ingredients and quantities.)

- Calories: 400
- Protein: 25g
- Fat: 18g
- Carbohydrates: 35g
- Fiber: 7g
- Sugar: 10g
- Sodium: 300mg

PROSCIUTTO PIZZA WITH CORN & ARUGULA

Prep Time: 15 minutes
Cook Time: 15 minutes
Serves: 4

Ingredients:

- 1 pound pizza dough, homemade or store-bought
- Olive oil for brushing
- 1 cup shredded mozzarella cheese
- 4 slices prosciutto
- One cup of fresh or, if frozen, thawed corn kernels
- 1 cup arugula, washed and dried
- Balsamic glaze for drizzling (optional)
- Salt and black pepper to taste

Directions:

1. Set the oven temperature to what your pizza dough recommends.
2. Roll out the pizza dough to the ideal thickness.
3. Place the rolled-out dough onto a parchment paper-lined baking sheet or pizza stone.
4. Use olive oil to lightly coat the dough's surface.
5. Evenly distribute the mozzarella shreds across the pizza dough.
6. Tear the prosciutto into smaller pieces and distribute them over the cheese.
7. Scatter the corn kernels over the pizza.
8. Bake in a preheated oven, following the pizza dough's instructions, until the cheese has melted and the crust is golden brown.
9. Take the pizza out of the oven and sprinkle some fresh arugula on top.
10. To taste, add salt and black pepper for seasoning.
11. Drizzle balsamic glaze over the top for extra flavor.
12. Slice and serve the Prosciutto Pizza with Corn & Arugula immediately.

Nutrition Information (per serving)

(Note: Nutritional values are approximate and may vary based on specific ingredients and quantities.)

- Calories: 350
- Protein: 15g
- Fat: 12g
- Carbohydrates: 45g
- Fiber: 3g
- Sugar: 2g
- Sodium: 600mg

EGGPLANT PARMESAN

Prep Time: 30 minutes
Cook Time: 45 minutes
Serves: 4

Ingredients:

- Cut two big eggplants into 1/2-inch rounds after peeling them.
- 2 cups breadcrumbs
- 1 cup grated Parmesan cheese
- 3 large eggs, beaten
- 2 cups marinara sauce (store-bought or homemade)
- 2 cups shredded mozzarella cheese
- Fresh basil leaves for garnish (optional)
- Olive oil for frying

Directions:

1. Preheat the oven to 375°F (190°C).
2. After putting the eggplant slices in a sieve, salt them. Let them sit for fifteen to twenty minutes to remove extra moisture.
3. Use paper towels to wipe dry the eggplant slices after rinsing them in cold water.
4. In one shallow dish, place the breadcrumbs. In another dish, combine the grated Parmesan cheese and beaten eggs.
5. Press the breadcrumbs into each eggplant slice to help them stick by dipping them first in the egg mixture and then in the breadcrumbs.
6. Heat the oil made from olives in a big pan over medium-high heat. Slices of breaded eggplant should be fried in batches until both sides are golden brown. To remove any leftover oil, place them on paper towels.
7. Drizzle a little amount of marinara sauce over a baking dish. Arrange a layer of fried eggplant slices over the sauce.
8. Drizzle some mozzarella shreds on top of the eggplant layer. Continue layering the ingredients until all are utilized, and then top with a layer of mozzarella.
9. Bake in the oven for 30-35 minutes or until the cheese is melted and bubbly.

10. Take it out of the oven, rest for a few minutes, and then, if you'd like, top it with fresh basil leaves.

Nutrition Information (per serving)

(Note: Nutritional values are approximate and may vary based on specific ingredients and quantities.)

- Calories: 400
- Protein: 18g
- Fat: 20g
- Carbohydrates: 35g
- Fiber: 8g
- Sugar: 10g
- Sodium: 800mg

BBQ SHRIMP WITH GARLICKY KALE & PARMESAN-HERB COUSCOUS

Prep Time: 20 minutes
Cook Time: 20 minutes
Serves: 4

Ingredients:

For BBQ Shrimp:

- 1 pound large shrimp, peeled and deveined
- 2 tablespoons olive oil
- 2 cloves garlic, minced
- 1 teaspoon smoked paprika
- 1/2 teaspoon cayenne pepper
- Salt and black pepper to taste
- 1/4 cup BBQ sauce

For Garlicky Kale:

- One bunch of kale, cut with the stems removed
- 2 tablespoons olive oil
- 3 cloves garlic, minced
- Salt and black pepper to taste
- Lemon wedges for serving

For Parmesan-Herb Couscous:

- 1 cup couscous
- 1/4 cup chicken or veggie broth

- 1/4 cup grated Parmesan cheese
- Two tablespoons of finely chopped fresh herbs, such as thyme and parsley
- Salt and black pepper to taste

Directions:

1. BBQ Shrimp:

- Mix shrimp, olive oil, smoked paprika, minced garlic, cayenne pepper, salt, and black pepper in a bowl. Toss to coat the shrimp evenly.
- Turn the heat up to medium-high in a skillet. Add the marinated ones when the shrimp becomes pink and cook for two to three minutes on each side.
- Coat the shrimp with BBQ sauce, tossing to ensure they are well-coated, and cook for one to two minutes.
- *Garlicky Kale:*
- Place olive oil in a different pan and heat it to medium. Garlic, when minced, should be sautéed for 30 seconds or until aromatic.
- Add chopped kale to the pan, season with salt and black pepper, and sauté until the kale is wilted and tender. Squeeze lemon juice over the kale and toss.

2. Parmesan-Herb Couscous:

- Bring the broth to a boil in a saucepan. Turn off the heat, cover, and add the couscous. Give it five minutes to sit.
- Fluff the couscous with a fork. Add grated Parmesan cheese, chopped herbs, salt, and black pepper. Toss to combine.

3. Serve:

- Plate the BBQ Shrimp over a bed of Garlicky Kale and serve alongside Parmesan-Herb Couscous.
- Garnish with additional herbs and lemon wedges.

Nutrition Information (per serving)

(Note: Nutritional values are approximate and may vary based on specific ingredients and quantities.)

- Calories: 450

- Protein: 28g
- Fat: 14g
- Carbohydrates: 50g
- Fiber: 6g
- Sugar: 6g
- Sodium: 800mg

MEDITERRANEAN CHICKEN

Prep Time: 15 minutes
Cook Time: 25 minutes
Serves: 4

Ingredients:

- 4 boneless, skinless chicken breasts
- Salt and black pepper to taste
- 2 teaspoons dried oregano
- 1 teaspoon dried thyme
- 1 teaspoon smoked paprika
- 2 tablespoons olive oil
- 4 cloves garlic, minced
- 1 cup cherry tomatoes, halved
- Half a cup of sliced and pitted Kalamata olives
- 1/4 cup crumbled feta cheese
- Fresh parsley for garnish
- Lemon wedges for serving

Directions:

1. Preheat the oven to 400°F (200°C).
2. Season the chicken breasts with salt, black pepper, dried thyme, oregano, and smoky paprika on both sides.
3. Heat the olive oil in a skillet that is ovensafe to medium-high heat. The chicken breasts should be added and seared on each side for three to four minutes or until golden brown.
4. Add minced garlic to the skillet and sauté for 1 minute until fragrant.
5. Scatter halved cherry tomatoes and sliced Kalamata olives around the chicken in the skillet.
6. After transferring the skillet to the oven, warm it and bake the chicken for 16 to 20 minutes.
7. Take the pan out of the oven and sprinkle some feta cheese crumbles over the chicken.

8. Add some fresh parsley to the Mediterranean Chicken's garnish and serve it hot with lemon wedges.

Nutrition Information (per serving)

(Note: Nutritional values are approximate and may vary based on specific ingredients and quantities.)

- Calories: 320
- Protein: 30g
- Fat: 16g
- Carbohydrates: 10g
- Fiber: 3g
- Sugar: 4g
- Sodium: 600mg

FETA, SPINACH & TOMATO STUFFED SALMON

Prep Time: 15 minutes
Cook Time: 20 minutes
Serves: 4

Ingredients:

- 4 salmon fillets
- Salt and black pepper to taste
- 2 tablespoons olive oil
- 2 cups fresh spinach, chopped
- 1 cup cherry tomatoes, halved
- 1/2 cup feta cheese, crumbled
- 2 cloves garlic, minced
- 1 teaspoon dried oregano
- Lemon wedges for serving

Directions:

1. Preheat the oven to 375°F (190°C).
2. Add salt and black pepper to the salmon fillets' seasoning. Cut horizontally with a sharp knife to make a pocket in the middle of each fillet.
3. In a skillet, heat olive oil over medium heat. Add minced garlic and sauté for 1 minute until fragrant.
4. Cook the chopped spinach in the pan until it wilts. Take off the heat.
5. Mix the wilted spinach, halved cherry tomatoes, crumbled feta cheese, and dried oregano in a bowl.
6. Stuff each salmon fillet with the spinach, tomato, and feta mixture.
7. Arrange the filled salmon fillets onto a parchment paper-lined baking sheet.
8. Bake in the oven for 15-20 minutes or until the salmon is cooked and flakes easily.
9. Remove from the oven and serve the stuffed salmon hot, garnished with lemon wedges.

Nutrition Information (per serving)

(Note: Nutritional values are approximate and may vary based on specific ingredients and quantities.)

- Calories: 300
- Protein: 30g
- Fat: 18g
- Carbohydrates: 5g
- Fiber: 2g
- Sugar: 2g
- Sodium: 400mg

ROASTED TOMATOES

Prep Time: 10 minutes
Cook Time: 25 minutes
Serves: 4

Ingredients:

- 2 pounds cherry or grape tomatoes, halved
- 3 tablespoons olive oil
- 4 cloves garlic, minced
- 1 teaspoon dried oregano
- 1 teaspoon dried thyme
- Salt and black pepper to taste
- Fresh basil leaves for garnish (optional)

Directions:

1. Preheat the oven to 375°F (190°C).
2. Mix the chopped cherry or grape tomatoes, olive oil, minced garlic, salt, black pepper, dried oregano, and dried thyme in a big bowl. Make careful to coat the tomatoes well.
3. Spread the seasoned tomatoes evenly on a baking sheet lined with parchment paper.
4. Bake the tomatoes for 20 to 25 minutes or until tender and caramelize around the edges.
5. Remove from the oven and let them cool for a few minutes.
6. Garnish with fresh basil leaves if desired.
7. You may serve the roasted tomatoes as an appetizer, as a garnish for grilled bread, or as a tasty complement to pasta and salads.

Nutrition Information (per serving)

(Note: Nutritional values are approximate and may vary based on specific ingredients and quantities.)

- Calories: 100
- Protein: 2g

- Fat: 7g
- Carbohydrates: 10g
- Fiber: 2g
- Sugar: 6g
- Sodium: 10mg

ONE-PAN TUNA PASTA

Prep Time: 10 minutes
Cook Time: 15 minutes
Serves: 4

Ingredients:

- 8 oz (225g) pasta (spaghetti or your choice)
- 1 can (5 oz/140g) tuna, drained
- 2 tablespoons olive oil
- 1 small onion, finely chopped
- 2 cloves garlic, minced
- 1 can (14 oz/400g) diced tomatoes
- 1 teaspoon dried oregano
- 1 teaspoon dried basil
- Salt and black pepper to taste
- Red pepper flakes (optional for added heat)
- Fresh parsley for garnish
- Grated Parmesan cheese for serving

Directions:

1. Cook the pasta until al dente, following the directions on the package. After draining, set away.
2. In a large pan or skillet, heat olive oil over medium heat. Add chopped onions and sauté until softened.
3. Add the minced garlic and stir. Cook for a minute or two or until fragrant.
4. Pour in the diced tomatoes, dried oregano, dried basil, salt, black pepper, and red pepper flakes (if using). Stir to combine.
5. Let the tomato mixture simmer for 5-7 minutes, melding the flavors together.
6. Gently mix the drained tuna into the pan after adding it.
7. Include the cooked pasta in the pan and toss to incorporate and heat everything thoroughly.
8. Garnish with fresh parsley and serve hot. Optionally, sprinkle grated Parmesan cheese on top.

Nutrition Information (per serving)

(Note: Nutritional values are approximate and may vary based on specific ingredients and quantities.)

- Calories: 350
- Protein: 18g
- Fat: 8g
- Carbohydrates: 52g
- Fiber: 4g
- Sugar: 6g
- Sodium: 450mg

CAPRESE ASPARAGUS

Prep Time: 10 minutes
Cook Time: 15 minutes
Serves: 4

Ingredients:

- 1 lb (450g) fresh asparagus spears, trimmed
- 1 tablespoon olive oil
- Salt and black pepper to taste
- 1 cup cherry tomatoes, halved
- 1 cup fresh mozzarella balls (bocconcini), halved
- Balsamic glaze for drizzling
- Fresh basil leaves for garnish

Directions:

1. Preheat the oven to 400°F (200°C).
2. Place trimmed asparagus spears on a baking sheet. Drizzle with olive oil and season with salt and black pepper. Toss to coat evenly.
3. Roast the asparagus for 13 to 15 minutes or until it's crisp but still soft.
4. While the asparagus is roasting, prepare the cherry tomatoes and fresh mozzarella.
5. Once the asparagus is done, arrange it on a serving platter.
6. Scatter halved cherry tomatoes and mozzarella balls over the asparagus.
7. Drizzle the Caprese Asparagus with balsamic glaze.
8. Garnish with fresh basil leaves.
9. Serve immediately as a flavorful side dish.

Nutrition Information (per serving)

(Note: Nutritional values are approximate and may vary based on specific ingredients and quantities.)

- Calories: 150
- Protein: 8g
- Fat: 10g

- Carbohydrates: 10g
- Fiber: 4g
- Sugar: 4g
- Sodium: 200mg

FETA & HERB CRUSTED SALMON

Prep Time: 10 minutes
Cook Time: 15 minutes
Serves: 4

Ingredients:

- 4 salmon fillets (6 oz each)
- 1/2 cup crumbled feta cheese
- 2 tablespoons fresh parsley, chopped
- 1 tablespoon fresh dill, chopped
- 1 tablespoon olive oil
- 1 tablespoon Dijon mustard
- 1 teaspoon lemon zest
- Salt and black pepper to taste
- Lemon wedges for serving

Directions:

1. Preheat the oven to 400°F (200°C).
2. Combine crumbled feta, chopped parsley, dill, olive oil, Dijon mustard, lemon zest, salt, and black pepper in a small bowl. Mix until well combined.
3. Place the salmon fillets on a parchment paper-covered baking pan.
4. Spoon the feta and herb mixture evenly over each salmon fillet, pressing it gently to adhere.
5. Bake for 12 to 15 minutes or until a fork can easily pierce the salmon to test for doneness.
6. After the salmon is cooked, remove it from the oven and place it on serving dishes.
7. If wanted, garnish with more fresh herbs and serve with lemon wedges.

Nutrition Information (per serving)

(Note: Nutritional values are approximate and may vary based on specific ingredients and quantities.)

- Calories: 300

- Protein: 28g
- Fat: 18g
- Carbohydrates: 2g
- Fiber: 1g
- Sugar: 0g
- Sodium: 350mg

HALLOUMI SALAD

Prep Time: 15 minutes
Cook Time: 10 minutes
Serves: 4

Ingredients:

- 1 pack (8 oz/225g) halloumi cheese, sliced
- 4 cups mixed salad greens (arugula, spinach, lettuce)
- 1 cup cherry tomatoes, halved
- 1 cucumber, sliced
- 1 red bell pepper, thinly sliced
- 1/4 cup Kalamata olives, pitted
- 1/4 cup red onion, thinly sliced
- 1/4 cup fresh mint leaves, chopped
- 1/4 cup extra virgin olive oil
- 2 tablespoons balsamic vinegar
- 1 teaspoon Dijon mustard
- Salt and black pepper to taste

Directions:

1. Combine the mixed greens, cherry tomatoes, cucumber, red bell pepper, Kalamata olives, red onion, and fresh mint in a large salad bowl.
2. Cook the halloumi slices in a nonstick pan over medium heat for two to three minutes on each side or until golden brown.
3. While the halloumi is cooking, whisk together the olive oil, balsamic vinegar, Dijon mustard, salt, and black pepper in a small bowl to make the dressing.
4. Once the halloumi is done, remove it from the pan and let it cool for a minute.
5. Add the cooked halloumi to the salad.
6. Pour the salad with the dressing and gently toss to mix.
7. Serve the Halloumi Salad immediately, enjoying the warm, slightly melted halloumi with the crispness of the salad.

Nutrition Information (per serving)

(Note: Nutritional values are approximate and may vary based on specific ingredients and quantities.)

- Calories: 300
- Protein: 15g
- Fat: 25g
- Carbohydrates: 10g
- Fiber: 3g
- Sugar: 5g
- Sodium: 600mg

GIGANTES PLAKI (GREEK BAKED BEANS)

Prep Time: 15 minutes
Cook Time: 1 hour 30 minutes
Serves: 6

Ingredients:

- 2 cups dried giant white beans (gigantes), soaked overnight
- 1 large onion, finely chopped
- 3 cloves garlic, minced
- 1 can (14 oz) crushed tomatoes
- 1/2 cup extra virgin olive oil
- 1/4 cup fresh parsley, chopped
- 1 tablespoon tomato paste
- 1 teaspoon dried oregano
- 1 teaspoon ground cumin
- Salt and black pepper to taste
- 1/2 teaspoon red pepper flakes (optional)
- 2 cups water
- 1 lemon, juiced
- Lemon wedges and fresh parsley for garnish

Directions:

1. Preheat the oven to 350°F (175°C).
2. Drain the soaked beans and rinse them under cold water.
3. Place the beans in a big saucepan, cover with water, and bring to a boil. Once partly done, reduce heat and simmer for 20 to 25 minutes. Pour the beans.
4. In a separate pan, sauté the chopped onion in olive oil until translucent. Add minced garlic and continue to sauté for 1-2 minutes.
5. Add the tomato paste, oregano, cumin, salt, black pepper, red pepper flakes (if using), and the smashed tomatoes. Mix everything.
6. In a baking dish, place the partially cooked beans. Pour the tomato mixture over the beans.

7. Gently mix in the two cups of water in the baking dish.
8. Bake the dish for an hour in the oven with the foil covering it.
9. After 1 hour, remove the foil, add the lemon juice, and stir gently. Continue baking uncovered for 30 minutes or until the beans are tender and the top is golden.
10. Serve heated with lemon wedges and garnish with fresh parsley.

Nutrition Information (per serving)

(Note: Nutritional values are approximate and may vary based on specific ingredients and quantities.)

- Calories: 350
- Protein: 12g
- Fat: 14g
- Carbohydrates: 46g
- Fiber: 10g
- Sugar: 8g
- Sodium: 400mg

BAKED CHORIZO AND SQUASH RICE WITH MANCHEGO CRUST

Prep Time: 20 minutes
Cook Time: 40 minutes
Serves: 4

Ingredients:

- 1 cup Arborio rice
- 2 cups chicken or vegetable broth
- 1 tablespoon olive oil
- 1 onion, finely chopped
- 2 cloves garlic, minced
- 1/2 pound (225g) chorizo sausage, casing removed and crumbled
- 1 zucchini, diced
- 1 cup butternut squash, diced
- 1 teaspoon smoked paprika
- Salt and black pepper to taste
- 1/2 cup Manchego cheese, grated
- Fresh parsley, chopped (for garnish)

Directions:

1. Preheat the oven to 375°F (190°C).
2. Bring the vegetable or chicken broth to a boil in a medium saucepan. To keep it warm, turn down the heat to low.
3. Heat the olive oil in a large ovenproof skillet over medium heat. Add chopped onions and sauté until translucent.
4. Add minced garlic and crumbled chorizo to the skillet. Cook until the chorizo is browned.
5. Stir in Arborio rice and cook for 2-3 minutes until the rice is well-coated with the oil and begins to toast.
6. Add diced zucchini, butternut squash, smoked paprika, salt, and black pepper. Stir to combine.

7. Pour the warm broth over the rice and chorizo mixture. Stir well.
8. Put the skillet in the oven that has been warmed and cover it with a lid or foil.
9. Bake for 25-30 minutes or until the rice is cooked and the liquid is absorbed.
10. Remove the pan from the oven and cover the top with the shredded Manchego cheese.
11. Put the pan back in the oven and bake it for ten minutes, uncovered, or until the cheese gets a golden crust.
12. Garnish with fresh chopped parsley before serving.

Nutrition Information (per serving)

(Note: Nutritional values are approximate and may vary based on specific ingredients and quantities.)

- Calories: 380
- Protein: 14g
- Fat: 22g
- Carbohydrates: 30g
- Fiber: 3g
- Sugar: 2g
- Sodium: 900mg

SPICY MERGUEZ AND COD TRAY ROAST

Prep Time: 15 minutes
Cook Time: 25 minutes
Serves: 4

Ingredients:

- 4 cod fillets
- 1/2 pound (225g) merguez sausages, sliced
- 1 pound (450g) baby potatoes, halved
- 1 red bell pepper, sliced
- 1 yellow bell pepper, sliced
- 1 red onion, thinly sliced
- 2 tablespoons olive oil
- 2 teaspoons smoked paprika
- 1 teaspoon ground cumin
- 1 teaspoon ground coriander
- 1/2 teaspoon cayenne pepper (adjust to taste)
- Salt and black pepper to taste
- Fresh parsley, chopped (for garnish)

Directions:

1. Preheat the oven to 425°F (220°C).
2. Add the baby potatoes, cut in half, to a large mixing basin, sliced bell peppers, sliced red onion, olive oil, smoked paprika, ground cumin, ground coriander, cayenne pepper, salt, and black pepper. Toss to coat the vegetables evenly.
3. Spread the seasoned vegetables on a baking tray, creating an even layer.
4. Place the cod fillets on top of the vegetables.
5. Distribute the sliced merguez sausages around the cod fillets.
6. Roast in the oven for 20-25 minutes or until the cod is cooked and flakes easily with a fork.
7. Garnish with fresh chopped parsley before serving.

Nutrition Information (per serving)

(Note: Nutritional values are approximate and may vary based on specific ingredients and quantities.)

- Calories: 420
- Protein: 30g
- Fat: 20g
- Carbohydrates: 30g
- Fiber: 5g
- Sugar: 4g
- Sodium: 700mg

ITALIAN BAKED MEATBALLS

Prep Time: 15 minutes
Cook Time: 25 minutes
Serves: 4

Ingredients:

For the Meatballs:

- 1 pound (450g) ground beef
- 1/2 cup breadcrumbs
- 1/4 cup grated Parmesan cheese
- 1/4 cup fresh parsley, chopped
- 1 large egg
- 2 cloves garlic, minced
- 1 teaspoon dried oregano
- 1/2 teaspoon dried basil
- Salt and black pepper to taste

For the Tomato Sauce:

- 1 can (14 oz) crushed tomatoes
- 1 clove garlic, minced
- 1 teaspoon dried oregano
- 1/2 teaspoon dried basil
- Salt and black pepper to taste

For Serving:

- Cooked spaghetti or your preferred pasta
- Fresh basil, chopped (for garnish)
- Grated Parmesan cheese

Directions:

1. Preheat the oven to 400°F (200°C).

2. Combine ground beef, breadcrumbs, grated Parmesan, chopped parsley, egg, minced garlic, dried oregano, dried basil, salt, and black pepper in a large mixing bowl. Mix until well combined.
3. Shape the mixture into meatballs, about 1 to 1.5 inches in diameter, and place them on a baking sheet lined with parchment paper.
4. To make the tomato sauce, combine crushed tomatoes, minced garlic, dried basil, dried oregano, salt, and black pepper in a different bowl.
5. Spoon the tomato sauce over each meatball.
6. Bake in the preheated oven for 20-25 minutes or until the meatballs are cooked and browned on the outside.
7. While the meatballs are baking, cook spaghetti or your preferred pasta according to package instructions.
8. Serve the baked meatballs over cooked pasta. Add grated Parmesan cheese and freshly cut basil as garnishes.

Nutrition Information (per serving, excluding pasta)

(Note: Nutritional values are approximate and may vary based on specific ingredients and quantities.)

- Calories: 300
- Protein: 25g
- Fat: 18g
- Carbohydrates: 10g
- Fiber: 2g
- Sugar: 4g
- Sodium: 500mg

LAMB TAGINE

Prep Time: 15 minutes
Cook Time: 2 hours
Serves: 4

Ingredients:

- 1.5 pounds (700g) of lamb stew meat, cubed
- 2 tablespoons olive oil
- 1 large onion, finely chopped
- 3 cloves garlic, minced
- 1 teaspoon ground cumin
- 1 teaspoon ground coriander
- 1 teaspoon ground cinnamon
- 1 teaspoon ground ginger
- 1/2 teaspoon paprika
- 1/2 teaspoon turmeric
- 1/2 teaspoon cayenne pepper (adjust to taste)
- Salt and black pepper to taste
- 1 can (14 oz) diced tomatoes, undrained
- 1/2 cup dried apricots, halved
- 1/4 cup raisins
- 1 cup beef or vegetable broth
- 2 tablespoons honey
- Zest of 1 lemon
- Fresh cilantro, chopped (for garnish)
- Cooked couscous or rice (for serving)

Directions:

1. Heat the olive oil over medium heat in a large tagine or heavy-bottomed saucepan. When the onions are tender, add them diced and sauté.
2. Add minced garlic and cubed lamb to the pot. Brown the lamb on all sides.

3. Add ground cumin, coriander, cinnamon, ginger, paprika, turmeric, cayenne pepper, salt, and black pepper to the pot. To uniformly cover the meat with the seasonings, stir.
4. Pour in diced tomatoes with their juice, dried apricots, raisins, beef or vegetable broth, honey, and lemon zest. Stir to combine.
5. Simmer the mixture for a short while before turning down the heat. Once the lamb is cooked and the flavors have blended, cover and simmer for one to two hours.
6. Check the seasoning and adjust with more salt or pepper if needed.
7. Serve the lamb tagine over cooked couscous or rice. Garnish with fresh chopped cilantro.

Nutrition Information (per serving, excluding couscous or rice)

(Note: Nutritional values are approximate and may vary based on specific ingredients and quantities.)

- Calories: 450
- Protein: 30g
- Fat: 20g
- Carbohydrates: 40g
- Fiber: 5g
- Sugar: 25g
- Sodium: 600mg

CHICKEN PARMESAN

Prep Time: 15 minutes
Cook Time: 25 minutes
Serves: 4

Ingredients:

For the Breaded Chicken:

- 4 boneless, skinless chicken breasts
- 1 cup breadcrumbs
- 1/2 cup grated Parmesan cheese
- 2 teaspoons dried Italian seasoning
- Salt and black pepper to taste
- 2 large eggs, beaten
- 1/2 cup all-purpose flour
- Olive oil for frying

For the Tomato Sauce:

- 1 can (14 oz) crushed tomatoes
- 2 cloves garlic, minced
- 1 teaspoon dried oregano
- 1 teaspoon dried basil
- Salt and black pepper to taste

For Assembling:

- 1 cup shredded mozzarella cheese
- 1/4 cup grated Parmesan cheese
- Fresh basil or parsley for garnish

Directions:

1. Breaded Chicken:

- Preheat the oven to 375°F (190°C).

- Mix breadcrumbs, grated Parmesan, dried Italian seasoning, salt, and black pepper in a shallow dish.
- Coat each chicken breast in the breadcrumb mixture, pressing lightly to adhere, after dredging it in flour and dipping it in beaten eggs.
- In a large skillet, heat olive oil over medium-high heat. Once golden brown, fry the breaded chicken breasts on each side for three to four minutes. To drain excess oil, transfer to a plate lined with paper towels.

2. Tomato Sauce:

- Combine crushed tomatoes, minced garlic, dried oregano, dried basil, salt, and black pepper in a saucepan. Simmer for 10-15 minutes, stirring occasionally.

3. Assembling:

- Evenly cover the bottom of a baking dish with tomato sauce. On top, put the breaded chicken breasts.
- Spoon more tomato sauce over each chicken breast.
- Top with a sprinkle of grated Parmesan and shredded mozzarella.
- Bake in the oven for 20-25 minutes or until the cheese is melted and bubbly.
- Garnish with fresh basil or parsley before serving.

Nutrition Information (per serving)

(Note: Nutritional values are approximate and may vary based on specific ingredients and quantities.)

- Calories: 450
- Protein: 40g
- Fat: 20g
- Carbohydrates: 25g
- Fiber: 3g
- Sugar: 5g
- Sodium: 800mg

MEDITERRANEAN TILAPIA

Prep Time: 15 minutes
Cook Time: 20 minutes
Serves: 4

Ingredients:

- 4 tilapia fillets
- 2 tablespoons olive oil
- 2 cloves garlic, minced
- 1 teaspoon dried oregano
- 1 teaspoon dried thyme
- 1 teaspoon paprika
- 1/2 teaspoon cumin
- Salt and black pepper to taste
- Juice of 1 lemon
- 1 cup cherry tomatoes, halved
- 1/2 cup pitted and sliced Kalamata olives
- 1/4 cup crumbled feta cheese
- Fresh parsley, chopped (for garnish)

Directions:

1. Preheat the oven to 375°F (190°C).
2. After using a paper towel to pat dry, put the tilapia fillets in a baking dish.
3. In a small bowl, combine olive oil, minced garlic, cumin, paprika, dried oregano, thyme, salt, and black pepper.
4. Brush the olive oil mixture over the tilapia fillets.
5. Squeeze lemon juice over the fillets and scatter cherry tomatoes and Kalamata olives around them.
6. Bake in the oven for 18-20 minutes or until the tilapia is cooked and flakes easily with a fork.
7. Sprinkle crumbled feta cheese over the top during the last 5 minutes of baking.
8. Garnish with chopped fresh parsley before serving.

Nutrition Information (per serving)

(Note: Nutritional values are approximate and may vary based on specific ingredients and quantities.)

- Calories: 220
- Protein: 30g
- Fat: 10g
- Carbohydrates: 5g
- Fiber: 2g
- Sugar: 2g
- Sodium: 450mg

FAVORITE MEAT LOAF GYROS

Prep Time: 15 minutes
Cook Time: 45 minutes
Serves: 4

Ingredients:

For the Meat Loaf:

- 1 pound ground lamb
- 1/2 pound ground beef
- 1/2 cup breadcrumbs
- 1 small onion, finely chopped
- 2 cloves garlic, minced
- 1 teaspoon dried oregano
- 1 teaspoon ground cumin
- Salt and black pepper to taste
- 1 large egg
- 1/4 cup milk

For the Tzatziki Sauce:

- 1 cup Greek yogurt
- 1 cucumber, peeled, seeded, and finely diced
- 2 cloves garlic, minced
- 1 tablespoon fresh dill, chopped
- 1 tablespoon fresh mint, chopped
- Salt and black pepper to taste

For Serving:

- Pita bread
- Sliced tomatoes
- Sliced red onions
- Fresh lettuce

Directions:

1. Meat Loaf:

- Preheat the oven to 375°F (190°C).
- Combine ground lamb, beef, breadcrumbs, chopped onion, minced garlic, dried oregano, ground cumin, salt, black pepper, egg, and milk in a large bowl. Mix until well combined.
- Shape the meat mixture into a loaf and place it on a baking sheet.
- Bake in the oven for 40-45 minutes until 160°F (71°C) is reached within.
- Let the meatloaf rest for a few minutes before slicing.

2. Tzatziki Sauce:

1. Mix Greek yogurt, diced cucumber, minced garlic, chopped dill, chopped mint, salt, and black pepper in a bowl.
2. Refrigerate the tzatziki sauce for at least 30 minutes before serving.

3. Assembling Gyros:

1. Warm the pita bread.
2. Spread a generous spoonful of tzatziki sauce on each pita.
3. Add slices of meatloaf, tomatoes, red onions, and lettuce.
4. Fold the pita to form a gyro.

Nutrition Information (per serving)

(Note: Nutritional values are approximate and may vary based on specific ingredients and quantities.)

- Calories: 550
- Protein: 35g
- Fat: 28g
- Carbohydrates: 40g
- Fiber: 4g
- Sugar: 6g
- Sodium: 800mg

MEDITERRANEAN TOMATO BITES

Prep Time: 15 minutes
Cook Time: 0 minutes (No cooking required)
Serves: 4

Ingredients:

- 2 large tomatoes, sliced into rounds
- 1/2 cup crumbled feta cheese
- 1/4 cup pitted and sliced Kalamata olives
- 2 tablespoons fresh basil, chopped
- 1 tablespoon extra-virgin olive oil
- 1 teaspoon balsamic glaze (optional)
- Salt and black pepper to taste

Directions:

1. Arrange the tomato slices onto a dish for presentation.
2. Sprinkle crumbled feta cheese over each tomato round.
3. Scatter sliced Kalamata olives on top of the feta.
4. Drizzle extra-virgin olive oil over the tomato bites.
5. Sprinkle chopped fresh basil over the top.
6. If desired, drizzle a bit of balsamic glaze for added flavor.
7. To taste, add salt and black pepper for seasoning.
8. Serve immediately and enjoy!

Nutrition Information (per serving)

(Note: Nutritional values are approximate and may vary based on specific ingredients and quantities.)

- Calories: 90
- Protein: 3g
- Fat: 7g
- Carbohydrates: 5g

- Fiber: 2g
- Sugar: 3g
- Sodium: 200mg

Chapter 5: Desserts and Sweets

LOUKOUMADES – GREEK HONEY BALLS

Prep Time: 20 minutes
Cook Time: 20 minutes
Serves: 6-8

Ingredients:

For the Dough:

- 2 cups all-purpose flour
- 1 teaspoon active dry yeast
- 1 teaspoon sugar
- 1/2 teaspoon salt
- 1 1/2 cups warm water

For Frying:

- Vegetable oil for deep frying

For Syrup:

- 1 cup honey
- 1/2 cup water
- 1 cinnamon stick
- Zest of 1 orange

For Serving:

- Chopped nuts (e.g., walnuts, pistachios)
- Cinnamon for sprinkling

Directions:

1. Dough:

- Mix sugar, active dry yeast, and warm water in a bowl. Until it foams, let it sit for five to ten minutes.
- In a large mixing bowl, combine the flour and salt. Make a well in the center and pour in the yeast mixture.

- Mix well until you have a smooth batter. The batter should warmly rise for one to two hours, or until it has doubled, in the basin covered with a kitchen towel.

2. Frying:

- Preheat vegetable oil to 350°F (175°C) in a deep fryer or heavy-bottomed saucepan.
- Drop little bits of dough into the heated oil using two spoons or an ice cream scoop. Fry until crispy and golden brown, rotating once a few minutes to provide uniform frying. Each batch typically takes two to three minutes.
- To absorb extra oil, take the loukoumades out of the oil and put them on a dish covered with paper towels.

3. Syrup:

- Combine honey, water, cinnamon stick, and orange zest in a saucepan. Over medium heat, bring the mixture to a simmer, stirring from time to time.
- Simmer it for around five minutes to let the flavors combine. Take off the heat and throw away the orange zest and cinnamon stick.

4. Assembly:

- Dip the fried loukoumades into the warm honey syrup, ensuring they are well coated.
- Arrange the honey-soaked loukoumades on a serving platter.
- Sprinkle with chopped nuts and a dash of cinnamon.
- Serve immediately and enjoy these delicious Greek honey balls!

Nutrition Information (per serving)

(Note: Nutritional values are approximate and may vary based on specific ingredients and quantities.)

- Calories: 320
- Protein: 4g
- Fat: 2g
- Carbohydrates: 74g
- Fiber: 2g
- Sugar: 40g
- Sodium: 160mg

BEST TAHINI BROWNIES

Prep Time: 15 minutes
Cook Time: 25 minutes
Serves: 12

Ingredients:

- 1/2 cup tahini
- 1/2 cup unsalted butter, melted
- 1 cup granulated sugar
- 2 large eggs
- 1 teaspoon vanilla extract
- 1/2 cup all-purpose flour
- 1/4 cup unsweetened cocoa powder
- 1/4 teaspoon salt
- 1/2 cup chocolate chips (optional)
- 1/4 cup chopped nuts (walnuts or almonds), optional

Directions:

1. Set the oven's temperature to 175°C/350°F. Grease a square baking pan, then line it with parchment paper, allowing an overhang for simple removal.
2. Whisk together melted butter, tahini, and sugar in a mixing bowl until well combined.
3. Beat thoroughly after adding each egg, one at a time. Add the vanilla essence and stir.
4. In another dish, sift the flour, salt, and cocoa powder.
5. Add the wet and dry ingredients gradually and stir just until mixed. Take caution not to blend too much.
6. If desired, fold in chocolate chips and chopped nuts into the batter.
7. Evenly distribute the brownie batter into the pan that has been prepared.
8. Bake for 25 to 30 minutes in a preheated oven or until a toothpick inserted in the center comes out slightly moistened with crumbs.
9. After the brownies have cooled in the pan for ten minutes, remove them using the overhanging parchment paper and allow them to rest entirely on a wire rack.

Nutrition Information (per serving)

(Note: Nutritional values are approximate and may vary based on specific ingredients and quantities.)

- Calories: 220
- Protein: 3g
- Fat: 14g
- Carbohydrates: 23g
- Fiber: 1g
- Sugar: 16g
- Sodium: 50mg

OLIVE OIL CAKE

Prep Time: 15 minutes
Cook Time: 40-45 minutes
Serves: 8-10

Ingredients:

- 1 1/2 cups all-purpose flour
- 1 cup granulated sugar
- 1/2 teaspoon baking powder
- 1/4 teaspoon baking soda
- 1/4 teaspoon salt
- 3 large eggs, room temperature
- 1 cup extra-virgin olive oil
- 1 cup whole milk, room temperature
- 1 teaspoon vanilla extract
- Zest of 1 lemon
- Powdered sugar for dusting (optional)

Directions:

1. Set the oven's temperature to 175°C/350°F. Butter and dust a 9-inch circular cake pan.
2. Mix flour, sugar, baking soda, baking powder, and salt in a large bowl.
3. Beat the eggs in another basin until they become pale and slightly thickened.
4. Beat the eggs until thoroughly blended, then gradually add the olive oil.
5. Add the wet and dry ingredients in three batches, switching out the milk. With the dry ingredients, start and finish. Blend until barely mixed.
6. Stir in the zest of lemon and vanilla essence.
7. Using a spatula, level the top of the batter after pouring it into the prepared cake pan.
8. Bake in the oven for 40-45 minutes or until a toothpick inserted into the center comes clean.
9. After the cake has cooled in the pan for 10 minutes, transfer it to a wire rack to finish cooling.
10. Dust the cooled cake with powdered sugar if desired before serving.

Nutrition Information (per serving)

(Note: Nutritional values are approximate and may vary based on specific ingredients and quantities.)

- Calories: 320
- Protein: 4g
- Fat: 20g
- Carbohydrates: 32g
- Fiber: 1g
- Sugar: 18g
- Sodium: 120mg

GREEK YOGURT PANNA COTTA

Prep Time: 10 minutes
Cook Time: 5 minutes (plus chilling time)
Serves: 4

Ingredients:

- 1 cup heavy cream
- 1/4 cup honey
- One tsp vanilla extract
- 1 packet (2 1/4 teaspoons) unflavored gelatin
- 2 tablespoons water
- 1 1/2 cups Greek yogurt
- Fresh berries for garnish (optional)
- Mint leaves for garnish (optional)

Directions:

1. In a saucepan, boil the heavy cream over medium heat until it simmers. Take off the heat.
2. Add the vanilla essence and honey, stirring until the honey dissolves completely.
3. Sprinkle the gelatin over the water in a small bowl and allow it to bloom for one minute.
4. Stir the blooming gelatin into the heated cream mixture until it dissolves completely.
5. Cool slightly before adding the Greek yogurt and whisking until thoroughly blended and creamy.
6. Divide the mixture among four ramekins or glasses.
7. The panna cotta should be chilled for four hours or more to solidify.
8. Garnish with mint leaves and fresh berries before serving.

Nutrition Information (per serving)

(Note: Nutritional values are approximate and may vary based on specific ingredients and quantities.)

- Calories: 250

- Protein: 7g
- Fat: 18g
- Carbohydrates: 17g
- Fiber: 0g
- Sugar: 15g
- Sodium: 35mg

BRÛLÉED RICOTTA

Prep Time: 10 minutes
Cook Time: 5 minutes
Serves: 4

Ingredients:

- 1 cup ricotta cheese
- 1/4 cup granulated sugar
- 1 teaspoon vanilla extract
- Fresh berries for topping
- 2 tablespoons brown sugar (for brûlée topping)

Directions:

1. Combine the ricotta cheese, granulated sugar, and vanilla extract in a bowl. Mix until well combined.
2. Divide the ricotta mixture among four serving dishes.
3. Smooth the surface of the ricotta in each dish.
4. Evenly scatter brown sugar on top of each dish with ricotta.
5. Using a kitchen torch, carefully torch the sugar until it melts and forms a golden-brown crust. If you don't have a kitchen torch, place the dishes under a broiler for 1-2 minutes until the sugar caramelizes.
6. Allow the brûléed ricotta to cool for a few minutes.
7. Top with fresh berries just before serving.

Nutrition Information (per serving)

(Note: Nutritional values are approximate and may vary based on specific ingredients and quantities.)

- Calories: 180
- Protein: 7g
- Fat: 8g
- Carbohydrates: 20g
- Fiber: 1g

- Sugar: 17g
- Sodium: 40mg

HONEYED PHYLLO STACKS WITH PISTACHIOS, SPICED FRUIT & YOGURT

Prep Time: 20 minutes
Cook Time: 10 minutes
Serves: 4

Ingredients:

- 8 sheets phyllo dough, thawed if frozen
- 1/2 cup unsalted butter, melted
- 1/4 cup honey
- 1 cup Greek yogurt
- One cup of mixed fresh fruit (figs, sliced peaches, or berries)
- 1/4 cup chopped pistachios
- 1 teaspoon ground cinnamon
- 1/2 teaspoon ground cardamom

Directions:

1. Preheat the oven to 375°F (190°C). Line a baking sheet with parchment paper.
2. Place one sheet of phyllo dough on a sanitized surface and gently brush it with melted butter. Stack one more sheet on top, and so on, to create four layers.
3. Cut the layered phyllo into squares or rectangles using a sharp knife.
4. Place the stacks of phyllo on the baking sheet that has been prepared, and bake for 8 to 10 minutes or until crispy and golden brown. Observe them closely to avoid burning them.
5. While the phyllo stacks are baking, mix the honey, cinnamon, and cardamom in a small bowl.
6. When the phyllo stacks are done, take them out of the oven and, while still warm, pour the honey mixture over them.
7. Allow the phyllo stacks to cool slightly.
8. To assemble, layer the honeyed phyllo stacks with Greek yogurt, mixed fresh fruits, and chopped pistachios.
9. Serve immediately and enjoy!

Nutrition Information (per serving)

(Note: Nutritional values are approximate and may vary based on specific ingredients and quantities.)

- Calories: 350
- Protein: 8g
- Fat: 20g
- Carbohydrates: 38g
- Fiber: 3g
- Sugar: 20g
- Sodium: 150mg

STICKY GLUTEN-FREE LEMON CAKE

Prep Time: 15 minutes
Cook Time: 35 minutes
Serves: 8

Ingredients:

For the Cake:

- 1 1/2 cups gluten-free flour
- 1 teaspoon baking powder
- 1/2 teaspoon baking soda
- 1/4 teaspoon salt
- 1/2 cup unsalted butter, softened
- 1 cup granulated sugar
- 2 large eggs
- 1 teaspoon vanilla extract
- Zest of 2 lemons
- 1/2 cup buttermilk

For the Sticky Lemon Glaze:

- Juice of 2 lemons
- 1/2 cup powdered sugar

Directions:

1. Set oven temperature to 350°F, or 180°C. Grease and line a circular cake pan (8 inches/20 cm) with parchment paper.
2. Whisk together the gluten-free flour, baking powder, baking soda, and salt in a bowl. Set aside.
3. In a large mixing basin, beat the granulated sugar and softened butter until light and creamy.
4. One egg at a time, adding and beating well after each addition. Add the lemon zest and vanilla essence and stir.
5. Buttermilk should be added in intervals as you gradually mix the dry components with the wet ones. With the dry ingredients, start and finish. Blend until barely mixed.

6. Pour the batter into the prepared cake pan and smooth the top.
7. When a toothpick in the center comes out clean, bake for 30 to 35 minutes.
8. Make the sticky lemon glaze while the cake bakes. Mix powdered sugar and lemon juice in a small bowl until well blended.
9. Once the cake is done, remove it from the oven and immediately poke several holes in the top using a skewer or fork.
10. Pour the sticky lemon glaze over the warm cake, allowing it to soak in.
11. After letting the cake set in the pan for fifteen minutes, turn it onto a wire rack to finish cooling.

Nutrition Information (per serving)

(Note: Nutritional values are approximate and may vary based on specific ingredients and quantities.)

- Calories: 320
- Protein: 3g
- Fat: 15g
- Carbohydrates: 45g
- Fiber: 1g
- Sugar: 28g
- Sodium: 180mg

RED FRUIT SALAD WITH LEMON-VANILLA BEAN SYRUP

Prep Time: 15 minutes
Cook Time: 5 minutes
Serves: 4

Ingredients:

For the Fruit Salad:

- 2 cups fresh strawberries, hulled and halved
- 1 cup fresh raspberries
- 1 cup fresh pomegranate arils
- 1 cup red grapes, halved
- Mint leaves for garnish (optional)

For the Lemon-Vanilla Bean Syrup:

- 1/2 cup granulated sugar
- 1/2 cup water
- Zest of 1 lemon
- Juice of 1 lemon
- 1 vanilla bean, split lengthwise

Directions:

1. Combine the strawberries, raspberries, pomegranate arils, and red grapes in a large mixing bowl. Gently toss the fruits together.
2. Mix sugar, water, lemon zest, lemon juice, and the scraped vanilla bean seeds in a small saucepan.
3. Bring the syrup mixture to a simmer over medium heat, stirring until the sugar dissolves. Allow it to simmer for 2-3 minutes to infuse the flavors.
4. After taking the syrup off the stove, give it some time to cool.
5. To eliminate the leftover vanilla bean and lemon zest, strain the syrup. Let the syrup cool down.

6. Drizzle the lemon-vanilla bean syrup over the red fruit salad and toss gently to coat the fruits.
7. Place the fruit salad in the refrigerator for at least half an hour before serving to enable the flavors to mingle.
8. Garnish with fresh mint leaves if desired, and serve chilled.

Nutrition Information (per serving)

(Note: Nutritional values are approximate and may vary based on specific ingredients and quantities.)

- Calories: 120
- Protein: 1g
- Fat: 0g
- Carbohydrates: 30g
- Fiber: 4g
- Sugar: 24g
- Sodium: 5mg

CREMA CATALANA

Prep Time: 20 minutes
Cook Time: 10 minutes + chilling time
Serves: 4

Ingredients:

- 2 cups whole milk
- Zest of 1 orange
- 1 cinnamon stick
- 4 large egg yolks
- 1/2 cup granulated sugar
- 2 tablespoons cornstarch
- 1 teaspoon vanilla extract
- 2 tablespoons brown sugar (for caramelizing the top)

Directions:

1. Heat the milk in a saucepan with the orange zest and cinnamon stick over medium heat. After bringing it to a simmer, turn off the heat and steep it for fifteen minutes. Strain the milk to remove the zest and cinnamon sticks.
2. Mix the egg yolks, cornstarch, and granulated sugar in a dish.
3. Slowly pour the warm milk into the egg mixture, whisking continuously to avoid curdling.
4. Replacing the pot with the mixture, whisk constantly over medium heat until the liquid thickens. Five to seven minutes should pass.
5. Take the pot off the burner once it has thickened, and whisk in the vanilla essence.
6. Divide the custard among serving dishes or ramekins. Allow them to cool to room temperature, then refrigerate for at least 2 hours or until set.
7. Replacing the pot with the mixture, whisk constantly over medium heat until the liquid thickens. Five to seven minutes should pass.
8. Allow the caramelized sugar to harden for a minute before serving.

Nutrition Information (per serving)

(Note: Nutritional values are approximate and may vary based on specific ingredients and quantities.)

- Calories: 280
- Protein: 6g
- Fat: 10g
- Carbohydrates: 41g
- Fiber: 0g
- Sugar: 34g
- Sodium: 60mg

GALAKTOBOUREKO

Prep Time: 30 minutes
Cook Time: 1 hour + chilling time
Serves: 12

Ingredients:

For the Custard:

- 4 cups whole milk
- 1 cup semolina flour
- 1 cup granulated sugar
- 4 large eggs
- 1 teaspoon vanilla extract
- Zest of 1 lemon

For the Filo Layers:

- 1 package (16 ounces) filo dough, thawed
- 1 cup unsalted butter, melted

For the Syrup:

- 1 cup water
- 1 cup granulated sugar
- Juice of 1/2 lemon

Directions:

1. Prepare the Custard:

- Heat the milk over medium heat in a saucepan until it's warm but not boiling.
- Combine the sugar and semolina flour in a mixing dish. One by one, add the eggs, stirring well after each addition.
- Slowly pour the warm milk into the semolina mixture, whisking continuously.
- Put the mixture back in the pot and whisk continuously over medium heat until it thickens. It will take ten to fifteen minutes.
- Remove from heat, stir in the vanilla extract and lemon zest, and let the custard cool.

2. Assemble the Layers:

- Preheat the oven to 350°F (175°C).
- Melt the butter and brush a baking dish with it.
- Layer half of the filo sheets in the dish, brushing each with melted butter.
- Pour the cooled custard over the filo layers.
- Layer the remaining filo sheets, brushing each sheet with melted butter again.

3. Bake:

- Score the top layers of filo into serving-size pieces.
- Bake in the oven for about 45-50 minutes or until the top is golden brown.

4. Prepare the Syrup:

- While the Galaktoboureko is baking, combine water, sugar, and lemon juice in a saucepan. Once it reaches a boil, reduce the heat and let it gently simmer for 10 minutes.
- Let the syrup cool.

5. Finish and Serve:

- Cover the warm pastry with the cooled syrup after taking the Galaktoboureko out of the oven.
- Allow it to absorb the syrup and cool before cutting it into squares along the scored lines.

Nutrition Information (per serving)

(Note: Nutritional values are approximate and may vary based on specific ingredients and quantities.)

- Calories: 380
- Protein: 8g
- Fat: 18g
- Carbohydrates: 48g
- Fiber: 1g
- Sugar: 28g
- Sodium: 190mg

Printed in Great Britain
by Amazon